IT IS SO ORDERED

THE SUPREME COURT RULES ON SCHOOL SEGREGATION

IT IS

BY DANIEL M. BERMAN

SO ORDERED

THE SUPREME COURT RULES ON SCHOOL SEGREGATION

W · W · NORTON & COMPANY · INC ·
NEW YORK

FOR STUART AND ADRIANE

Library of Congress Catalog Card No. 66–11255

Published simultaneously in Canada by
George J. McLeod Limited, Toronto

| ISBN | 0 | 393 | 09679 | 3 | Cloth Edition |
| ISBN | 0 | 393 | 05259 | 1 | Paper Edition |

PRINTED IN THE UNITED STATES OF AMERICA

7 8 9 0

CONTENTS

PREFACE

The average American knows far more about the Executive Branch and about Congress than he does about the Supreme Court. Although the Court is, at least in theory, a coequal and coordinate branch of the Federal Government, it seems to command the attention of the press only when sensational public issues are decided or when the Justices themselves become the subject of public controversy. The same mass media that are packed with news of presidential and congressional actions provide only the most meager coverage of developments in the Supreme Court.

It is easy to understand why this is so. Although there are important exceptions, actions of the Supreme Court are not always recognized as having a direct and immediate impact on large numbers of people. The Court, after all, can act only when cases or controversies are brought before it in the normal course of litigation, and, at least in a technical sense, decisions in such matters have legal consequences only for the actual parties. In sharp contrast, presidential and congressional actions apply, more often than not, to large numbers of people. When a President decides, for example, to call the military reserve into active service, the lives of innumerable families may change in the twinkling of an eye. Similarly, an Act of Congress that increases the withholding tax takes money out of the pockets of millions of Americans almost overnight.

Press coverage of the Supreme Court is skimpy for another reason as well. Judicial opinions are formidable legal documents, often replete with references to other cases and to legal principles that may baffle a general-assignment reporter. And because legal writers are in short supply, only the most

vii

prosperous newspapers can afford to put a specialist on the Supreme Court "beat."

But despite the fact that it is only superficially understood by the general public, the Supreme Court is an institution so powerful that it was able in the course of one short decade to outlaw public school segregation, compel the fair apportionment of state legislatures, exclude religious ritual from the public schools, and expand dramatically the rights of those accused of crime.

Nowhere was the importance of Supreme Court decisions more evident than in the School Segregation Cases of 1954, for these cases, perhaps more than any other single factor, helped to inspire the massive Negro awakening that may prove to be an outstanding phenomenon of twentieth century American life.

It is with the School Segregation Cases that this book deals. Although a considerable amount of space is devoted to the substantive issue of educational segregation, the primary effort is to provide an outline of the federal judicial process. Thus the principal case that the Court decided on May 17, 1954, *Brown* v. *Board of Education,* serves as something of a vehicle for a discussion of the judicial system of the United States. If the reader also emerges with some knowledge of the law of race relations, that is a happy by-product—but a by-product nonetheless.

ACKNOWLEDGMENTS

A number of individuals have made generous contributions of both their time and their wisdom in the preparation of this book. Foremost among these are Mr. Bernard L. Sperling of Poughkeepsie, New York, and two of my colleagues at The American University, Dr. Robert E. Goostree, professor of law and government, and Dr. Louis S. Loeb, associate professor of government. Helpful suggestions came also from Mr. Edward C. Schade, assistant clerk of the Supreme Court of the United States; Mr. Banning E. Whittington, the Supreme Court's press officer; Commissioner Philip Elman of the Federal Trade Commission, who was author of the Government's main briefs in the School Segregation Cases; and Mr. Oliver W. Hill, now director of the Intergroup Relations Service of the Federal Housing Administration, who was one of the attorneys for the Negro children in the Virginia case.

Acknowledgment should be made of the assistance provided by the Norton advisory editor in American government, Professor Theodore J. Lowi of the University of Chicago. There was also help in the early stages of the work from Mr. Jacques De Puy, a former student of mine, and in the later stages from Mr. Rapheal Lewis, my graduate assistant at The American University.

Valuable clerical assistance was provided by Mrs. Françoise Yohalem, and photoduplication facilities were made available thanks to Mr. Paul W. Howerton, director of the Center for Technology and Administration at The American University.

No author has ever had a more intelligent, efficient, and cooperative secretarial assistant than Mrs. Marylee Buchly. In addition, my dean, Earl H. DeLong, deserves an expression of appreciation for helping to create a stimulating and invigorating atmosphere in which to work. And a constant inspiration was the teacher with whom I first studied political science, Dr. Edward McNall Burns, professor emeritus and former chairman of the Department of Political Science at Rutgers University.

Extremely perceptive stylistic criticism was provided by my wife Aline, who also deserves credit for being able to tolerate a grumpy disposition that is at its worst when its possessor is in the throes of composition.

IT IS SO ORDERED

THE SUPREME COURT RULES ON SCHOOL SEGREGATION

1. Introduction

On May 17, 1954, the Supreme Court held unanimously that the United States Constitution is violated when a state compels Negroes to attend racially segregated public schools. White Southerners reacted to the decision with a combination of frustration, resentment, anger, and resignation. Negroes, on the other hand, hailed the decision as a giant step toward a future of legal equality and full acceptance into American society. Both groups seemed to understand that the world they had known would no longer be the same.

It was not the first time in American history that judges had influenced the course of race relations. In 1857, a Supreme Court dominated by Southern members ruled in the Dred Scott case that Congress lacked the constitutional power to ban slavery even in the areas that were under the direct control of the Federal Government, and that legislation purporting to prohibit slavery violated the Fifth Amendment because it amounted to taking property without due process of law.[1]

---

[1] *Dred Scott* v. *Sandford*, 19 Howard 393 (1857). Only once before had the Supreme Court presumed to declare an Act of Congress unconstitutional. That was in the 1803 case of *Marbury* v. *Madison* (1 Cranch 137), when the principle of judicial review over federal legislation was first established. (Each of the first ninety volumes of Supreme Court opinions bears the name of the official reporter in charge of the compilation [e.g., Cranch, Howard, Dallas]. Later volumes are cited as "United States Reports," abbreviated "U.S.")

1

Never were the political consequences of a judicial decision easier to observe, for while the Court's action gladdened the hearts of Southern planters, it succeeded only in inflaming the North, and actually helped bring on the Civil War.

Yet the Dred Scott decision was not to be the last word on slavery, for the Civil War brought in its wake a demand that the Constitution be amended to provide Congress with the power that the original document had supposedly withheld. The result was the addition to the Constitution of the Thirteenth Amendment, which clearly and unambiguously outlawed the institution of slavery.[2] Shortly thereafter, two other "Civil War Amendments" were ratified. The first of these, the Fourteenth Amendment, had the immediate effect of making the Negro a citizen [3] and providing him in addition with a number of other protections: his "privileges and immunities" were not to be abridged by any state; he was not to be deprived of "life, liberty, or property, without due process of law"; and he was to enjoy in every state "the equal protection of the laws." The Fourteenth Amendment, moreover, provided that any state withholding the right to vote from the Negro would be punished by losing some of its seats in the House of Representatives. And the last of these Amendments, the Fifteenth, went even further on the subject of voting by flatly prohibiting disfranchisement "on account of race, color, or previous condition of servitude."

It fell to the Supreme Court to define and interpret some of the most important provisions of these three Amendments. Instead of doing so in the spirit of the Congress that had framed them, the Court proceeded to weaken one protection

[2] The Constitution has been amended to overcome a Supreme Court decision on only two other occasions in the entire history of the nation. The Eleventh Amendment, ratified in 1798, nullified the decision in *Chisholm* v. *Georgia* (2 Dallas, 419 [1793]) that a citizen could have access to the federal courts if he wanted to bring suit against another state. And in 1913 the Sixteenth Amendment upset the decision in *Pollack* v. *Farmers' Loan & Trust Co.* (157 U.S. 429 [1895]) by sanctioning the imposition of an unapportioned federal income tax.

[3] The Supreme Court had declared in the Dred Scott decision that the Framers of the Constitution had not considered Negroes to be citizens.

after another, through a series of far-reaching decisions.

First to be affected was the privileges and immunities clause of the Fourteenth Amendment. Only five years after the ratification of the Amendment, the Court ruled that Congress had not intended for this clause to protect the most fundamental civil rights, which were said to flow from state citizenship, but only the rights associated with federal citizenship, which, it was made clear, were far less basic.[4] A similar fate awaited both the due process clause of the Fourteenth Amendment and the provision that states would have their representation in Congress reduced if they practiced racial disfranchisement. Due process was converted into a shield to defend business against governmental regulation, and, to a lesser extent, a protection for defendants in criminal cases. As for the penalty provision of the Amendment, the Supreme Court remained silent when the lower federal courts decided only a few years ago that it was not for the Judiciary to curtail the representation of states in the House for disfranchising Negroes; enforcement was left to Congress [5]—and Congress has never chosen to act.

That left only one clause of the Fourteenth Amendment—equal protection [6]—and the Court chose to give this concept, too, the narrowest possible interpretation. Its attitude became clear as early as 1883, when it struck down a federal law resting in part on the equal protection clause. In passing that law—the Civil Rights Act of 1875—Congress had acted on the theory that any state which did not move to prevent racial discrimination in places of public accommodation was denying Negroes the equal protection of its laws and abridging their privileges and immunities as well. Accordingly, the House and Senate had enacted legislation making it a criminal offense to exclude Negroes from public places such as theaters and inns.

[4] *Slaughter-House Cases,* 16 Wallace 36 (1873).
[5] *Saunders* v. *Wilkins,* 152 F. 2d 235 (1945); *Dennis* v. *United States,* 171 F. 2d 986 (1948).
[6] ". . . nor [shall any state] deny to any person within its jurisdiction the equal protection of the laws."

But the Court had other ideas. It declared that, under the Fourteenth Amendment, Congress could act against discrimination only when it was practiced directly by the government of a state; there could be no federal legislative remedy against any kind of private discrimination.[7]

Since this decision meant that the coverage of the equal protection clause was limited to discrimination stemming from state action, the only question that remained was whether states would even be held to an exacting standard of nondiscrimination. The Court gave the definitive answer to that question in 1896, in the landmark case of *Plessy* v. *Ferguson*.[8]

Beginning of an Era

The issue in the Plessy case was whether a state could, in spite of the equal protection clause, require by law that passengers in railroad cars be segregated according to race. Louisiana had done just that, providing that Negroes be given accommodations which were "equal but separate." When the constitutionality of this segregation statute was challenged before the Supreme Court, it was held that equal protection had not been violated. The Fourteenth Amendment, the Court said, had not been intended to accord social equality to the Negro but only political equality.

All but one of the Justices subscribed to the opinion in *Plessy*. That one, however, compensated in sheer indignation for what he lacked in numerical support. Justice John Marshall Harlan[9] used the word "pernicious" to describe the decision announced by his colleagues. A "brand of servitude and degradation," he said, was being placed on the Negro, and the "thin disguise of 'equal' accommodations [could not] atone for the wrong this day done." Then came the most memorable words in his dissenting opinion: "Our Constitution is color

[7] *Civil Rights Cases*, 109 U.S. 3 (1883).
[8] 163 U.S. 537.
[9] Grandfather of the present Justice Harlan.

blind and neither knows nor tolerates classes among citizens."
Harlan added:

> In respect of civil rights, all citizens are equal before the law.
> The humblest is the peer of the most powerful. The law re-
> gards man as man, and takes no account of his surroundings
> or of his color when his civil rights as guaranteed by the su-
> preme law of the land are involved.

The Court had ruled otherwise, however, and the stamp
of judicial approval had been placed on racial segregation.
Such segregation was not yet widespread in the South and
where it did exist it was of recent vintage. What the Court
had done was not so much to sanction an existing practice as
to put forth the idea for a new one.[10] The result was that under
the protective umbrella of the Plessy doctrine racial segregation came to dominate virtually all areas of Southern life.

One of the most important of these areas was education.
Even before 1896, segregated schools had existed in certain
areas, some of them in the North. The author of the majority
opinion in Plessy had actually been able to point to the color
bar in education as the "most common instance" of legally
recognized segregation.[11] But if segregated public schools did
indeed exist here and there before 1896, they multiplied at an
impressive rate, especially in the South, after the Supreme
Court gave them the imprimatur of constitutionality.

Although "separate but equal"[12] was supposed to be the
criterion where segregated schools were maintained, "separate"
was taken far more seriously than "equal." Negroes had to

[10] The most cogent refutation of the belief that segregation of the
Negro has deep historical roots in the United States is C. Vann Woodward, The Strange Career of Jim Crow (New York: Oxford Press, 1957),
a study of the interests served by the imposition of racial segregation
after the abandonment of Reconstruction.

[11] In turn, the Supreme Court indicated thirty-one years later that
the Plessy doctrine was applicable to education. Gong Lum v. Rice, 275
U.S. 78 (1927).

[12] The Louisiana statute upheld in the Plessy case had required
"equal but separate" facilities. In general usage, however, the order of
the two adjectives was often reversed, and "separate but equal" became
the accepted formula.

settle for dilapidated buildings that were poorly ventilated, inadequately lighted, and miserably overcrowded. In rural areas especially, desks and chairs were crude and outmoded, and libraries, where they existed at all, left much to be desired. Even more important, many teachers were hopelessly unqualified for their task, for often they themselves had received only a rudimentary education in inferior schools.

As the years went by, however, a Supreme Court that was radically different from the one responsible for the Plessy doctrine began to show unmistakable signs of displeasure with this state of affairs. In a series of cases dealing with higher education, the "equal" requirement was tightened up. In 1938, for example, the Court ruled that it was not enough for Missouri to underwrite the tuition of a Negro student in an out-of-state law school; since the only law school within the state was at the University of Missouri, the student would have to be enrolled there.[13] And ten years later the Court held that just as a Negro could not be compelled to leave the state to obtain training which was available to white students on home grounds, neither could he be required to *postpone* his education; it was unreasonable for Oklahoma to expect a prospective student to wait until a new law school for Negroes was opened.[14]

Both these principles were laid down in cases that concerned a type of education in which the Justices were particularly interested: the training of lawyers. Still a third case involving legal education was to reach the Supreme Court, and this one proved to be the most important of all.

Intangible Factors

This case arose in Texas, where a separate law school for Negroes had been established by the state. The school was located within the boundaries of Texas and its facilities were immediately available, thus satisfying the requirements

[13] *Missouri* ex rel. *Gaines* v. *Canada*, 305 U.S. 337 (1938).
[14] *Sipuel* v. *Board of Regents of University of Oklahoma*, 332 U.S. 631 (1948).

laid down in the two recent Supreme Court decisions. In addition, there was no allegation that the facilities of the school were inadequate. Under such circumstances, the Court was presented with a golden opportunity to take a new look at the constitutionality of the "separate but equal" formula if it so desired, for if the Negro law school was indeed the equal of the white, the only question left was whether segregation in and of itself violated the Fourteenth Amendment. The Negro student who wanted to enroll in the white law school hoped that the Court would seize the opportunity and re-examine the Plessy doctrine. So did his counsel, Thurgood Marshall, director of the legal arm of the National Association for the Advancement of Colored People (NAACP). Marshall urged the Court to wait no longer and to repudiate specifically the "separate but equal" doctrine as applied to public education.

Although it turned out that the Justices were not ready to go quite that far, the unanimous decision they rendered in 1950 was the next-best thing, from the standpoint of the NAACP. In an opinion by Chief Justice Fred M. Vinson, they declared for the first time that, at least where legal training was concerned, mere equality of *tangible* facilities was in-sufficient, for inequality might still exist with respect to other factors "which are incapable of objective measurement but which make for greatness in a law school." Such factors in-cluded the "reputation of the faculty, experience of the ad-ministration, position and influence of the alumni, standing in the community, traditions and prestige." On that basis, said the Court, the Negro school was far from being on a par with the white.[15]

The intriguing question that was asked after the promul-gation of this new doctrine was whether it would ever be possible, as long as a segregated school system was maintained, to meet the Supreme Court's test and to demonstrate sub-

[15] *Sweatt* v. *Painter,* 339 U.S. 629 (1950). On the same day that it announced this decision, the Supreme Court also held that a state uni-versity could not segregate its one Negro student by assigning him sep-arate facilities in the school's dining room, library, and classrooms. *McLaurin* v. *Oklahoma State Regents,* 339 U.S. 637 (1950).

stantial equality of those factors "which are incapable of objective measurement." Would not the very fact of segregation rule out the possibility of achieving equality if intangibles, too, were to be considered?

Despite the direction in which the Court seemed to be moving, some Southern states thought that a conscientious program to equalize tangible facilities in elementary and secondary schools might still make the Justices hesitate to repudiate the doctrine of "separate but equal" altogether. Something of a crash program was accordingly instituted in certain areas of the South to save segregated schools. Impressive building programs became the order of the day, with a number of states actually spending more on Negro schools in the early 1950's than they did on white schools.[16] Governor James F. Byrnes of South Carolina, who had once been a Supreme Court Justice, made no effort to hide the motive: to minimize the possibility that the federal courts would "take matters out of the state's hands." [17] It was thus evident that strategy and tactics were involved, and not a sudden concern for the welfare of Negro children like Linda Carol Brown, of Topeka, Kansas.

[16] Whitney M. Young, Jr., *To Be Equal* (New York: McGraw-Hill, 1964), p. 103.
[17] Quoted in Alfred H. Kelly, "The School Desegregation Case," in John A. Garraty, ed., *Quarrels That Have Shaped the Constitution* (New York: Harper & Row, 1964), p. 256.

2. In the Lower Courts

Linda Carol Brown, an eight-year-old Negro girl, was a pupil in a segregated public elementary school in Topeka. Every morning she had to walk through a railroad yard to catch the bus that would take her to her school, twenty-one blocks away. The bus usually arrived at the school thirty minutes before classes began, and sometimes even on cold winter mornings the door of the schoolhouse would be locked. When it was cold, the child would clap her hands or jump up and down in an effort to keep warm.[1]

The little girl's father, Oliver Brown, came to the conclusion that this arrrangement was anything but satisfactory. There was, after all, another public elementary school only five blocks from the Brown home. Mr. Brown wondered whether the city really had the right to exclude his daughter from that nearby school simply on account of her race.

Topeka claimed to have a legal basis for maintaining a segregated educational system: a state law specifically authorizing cities with a population of more than 15,000 to establish separate schools for Negro and white students.[2] But Oliver Brown—and the parents of twelve other Negro children who joined him in filing a court suit against the Topeka Board of

[1] Transcripts of Records and File Copies of Briefs, 1954 (in United States Supreme Court Library).
[2] *Ibid.*

Education—knew that this was the beginning and not the end of the legal question. It was not enough for the city to cite the existence of a state law sanctioning the imposition of the color line in its schools, because that state law itself was null and void if it violated any provision of either the Kansas constitution or the Constitution of the United States. The Negroes advanced the argument that a federal constitutional provision was indeed being violated: Section 1 of the Fourteenth Amendment. The state, they said, was denying their children "the equal protection of the laws."

Since this argument involved an interpretation of the United States Constitution, Oliver Brown and those joining with him had the right to prosecute their case either in a federal court or in a state court.[3] In the belief that a federal court might be more sympathetic to their contention they decided to make use of that right. The court in which they filed suit was the United States District Court for the District of Kansas.

At the Trial Level

District Courts, which exist in each of the states and in the territories as well,[4] are the trial courts of the United States

---

[3] Under Article III of the Constitution, the jurisdiction of the federal courts covers cases presenting questions peculiarly national in character. These include cases hinging on an interpretation of the federal Constitution, as well as others "arising under . . . the Laws of the United States, and Treaties made . . . under their Authority. . . ." The federal jurisdiction also encompasses: (1) "Controversies to which the United States shall be a Party"; (2) "Controversies between two or more States"; (3) controversies "between Citizens of different States"; and (4) admiralty and maritime cases. Originally, Article III also gave the federal courts jurisdiction over "Controversies . . . between a State and Citizens of another State," but the Eleventh Amendment transferred this power to the state courts. There has been some support in recent years for also depriving the federal courts of the power to decide "Controversies . . . between Citizens of different States." Congress has already limited the exercise of the power to controversies in which at least $10,000 is involved.

[4] There is at least one District Court in every state regardless of

judicial system. As courts of "first instance," their character-istic function is to hear cases and render judgments. They do this by means of an adversary procedure in which the opposing parties present witnesses and offer other evidence. Findings of fact are made, sometimes by a judge and at other times by a jury, with the judge responsible for applying pertinent rules of law. Although these findings of fact cannot be challenged on appeal, the case as a whole can be taken to a higher court for the purpose of reviewing legal questions.

In most instances, trials in a District Court are conducted by a single judge.[5] After a decision is reached, the losing party

---

size. The larger states are divided into two or more federal judicial districts, each served by a District Court. There are altogether ninety-two District Courts, their jurisdiction covering the fifty states as well as the District of Columbia, Puerto Rico, the Canal Zone, Guam, and the Virgin Islands. In the last three territories, the District Courts have a slightly different status than in the rest of the United States.

[5] Like the judges of the Courts of Appeals and the Justices of the Supreme Court, district judges are surrounded by constitutional protections designed to insure their independence. For one thing, Article III of the Constitution provides that the compensation of federal judges "shall not be diminished during their continuance in office." Moreover, life tenure is provided so that judges need not be dependent on either the President or Congress for retaining their positions. Since judges do hold their offices "during good behavior," however, they can be removed from office through impeachment proceedings. These require a majority vote in the House of Representatives and a two-thirds vote in the Senate. Four federal judges have been ousted in this manner (and others have resigned while proceedings against them were still pending), but never a Supreme Court Justice.

One Justice, Samuel Chase, came perilously close, however. In 1805, Chase was the target of sharp criticism from the Jeffersonian Republicans, who resented not only his participation in the presidential campaign of John Adams but also the attacks he had made on them in the course of judicial proceedings and the enthusiasm with which he had applied the Sedition Law of 1798. His critics said that this partisan behavior amounted to the commission of "high crimes and misdemeanors," and for that the constitutional remedy is removal from office. Accordingly, the House voted to impeach (or formally charge) Justice Chase under Article III. In the Senate, however, Chase was spared conviction, but by the uncomfortably narrow margin of four votes. With the wisdom of hindsight, Jefferson called the impeachment of a Justice "a farce," and predicted that it would "not be tried again." History has borne out his prediction.

may prosecute an appeal as a matter of right in one of the eleven Courts of Appeals (with the exception that the Government may not appeal from an acquittal in a criminal case).

Appellate Courts

Each Court of Appeals has jurisdiction over one of the circuits, or geographical areas, into which the country is divided. The circuits vary widely in size. They range from the Ninth, which takes in nine Western states, to the one in the District of Columbia, which covers only a relatively small area (though in addition to local cases it gets many others involving agencies of the Federal Government). There is also some variation in the number of judges authorized by Congress for the various Courts of Appeals, depending on the amount of federal litigation that can be expected. In one respect, however, the Courts of Appeals are uniform. They all sit in multi-member groupings only, with at least three judges participating in each decision.[6]

The Courts of Appeals have existed only since 1891. When Congress first established the federal judicial system more than a century earlier, it had not provided for any courts with exclusively appellate responsibilities. Of the sixteen tribunals that it did create, the thirteen District Courts were to act only as trial courts, dealing with admiralty (or maritime) cases primarily; the three Circuit Courts were to perform a similar trial function in criminal cases and in civil cases where the opposing parties were citizens of different states, though they had limited appellate jurisdiction as well. Oddly enough, the Circuit Courts had no judges assigned to them on a permanent basis. Instead, their semi-annual sessions were conducted by panels consisting of two Supreme Court Justices, who engaged in "circuit riding" as part of their regular duties, and one district

---

[6] Cases occasionally arise in which a majority of the judges on a Court of Appeals decide that the proceedings should be conducted *en banc*, with all members taking part instead of a panel of only three.

judge. Although this system underwent some changes in the decades that followed, no permanent appellate courts were established until the end of the nineteenth century.[7]

In 1891, a major reform was introduced when Congress passed the Evarts Act, providing for the creation of Courts of Appeals. The principal purpose of this legislation was to lighten the burden on the Supreme Court by relieving it of the duty to decide cases important to no one besides the litigants. With respect to such cases, the new Courts of Appeals would have the responsibility of reviewing the decisions of district judges. Much the same purpose was behind another judicial reform law enacted thirty-four years later, when Congress gave the Supreme Court almost unlimited discretion in deciding whether to review decisions of the Courts of Appeals.[8]

Thus the usual procedure today is that cases are tried in District Courts, with the losing party entitled to a review by a Court of Appeals. The decision of that court is final, except in the rare instances when the Supreme Court agrees to grant a hearing.[9]

Three-Judge District Court

But the School Segregation Cases fell into a special class of litigation in which a different procedure is followed. That procedure, which has been established by Congress, calls for the convening of an unusual kind of District Court when an injunction is sought against the enforcement of a federal, state, or municipal law on the ground that it is repugnant to the United States Constitution. Congress has provided for such a case to be heard by a panel of three judges, one of whom must be selected from the Court of Appeals serving that

[7] A comprehensive history of federal judicial administration is Felix Frankfurter and James M. Landis, *The Business of the Supreme Court* (New York: Macmillan, 1928).

[8] That law, the "Judges' Bill" of 1925, is discussed on pp. 34–35.

[9] The discretionary power of the Supreme Court to decide whether to accept a case is described on pp. 35–36.

particular circuit, and the two others, usually from District Courts.[10] Appeals from the decision of a three-member court go directly to the Supreme Court without intermediate review.[11]

Since the Negro plaintiffs in Topeka were asking that enforcement of the state segregation law be enjoined as a violation of the equal protection clause of the Constitution, they applied to a district judge for the convening of a three-member court. On his recommendation, the chief judge of the Court of Appeals for the Tenth Circuit appointed the men who would hear the evidence and decide whether to grant an injunction.

The issues raised in Kansas were brought up almost concurrently in four other cases in various Southern and border regions. These cases, which were destined to be disposed of by the Supreme Court on the same day as the Brown case, arose in South Carolina, Virginia, Delaware, and the District of Columbia.

In each case, an unusual type of evidence was presented on behalf of the Negro children: testimony from social scientists to the effect that segregation often inflicted serious psychological harm on children subjected to it. In the South Carolina case, for example, expert witnesses told the court that because of racial separation Negro children were likely to develop tendencies toward escapism and withdrawal, as well as feelings of hostility and resentment. Moreover, it was said, their sense of self-esteem could easily be impaired, because the institutional arrangements within which they functioned were predicated on the assumption that they were

[10] The members of such a statutory court are chosen by the chief judge of the Court of Appeals that exercises appellate jurisdiction over the district. Length of service on the Court of Appeals determines who is to be chief judge, with the exception that any member over seventy is ineligible.

[11] The convening of a three-judge court, with direct appeal to the Supreme Court, is authorized not simply for injunction proceedings but also when it is necessary to review orders of the Interstate Commerce Commission as well as certain actions by the United States under the anti-trust laws and the interstate commerce laws.

ERNEST MANHEIM, having been first duly sworn, testified on behalf of the plaintiffs in rebuttal as follows:

Direct examination.

By Mr. Greenberg:

Q. Would you please state your full name to the Court.
A. Ernest Manheim.

Q. What is your occupation, Mr. Manheim?
A. Professor of Sociology at the University of Kansas City.

[fol. 343]   Q. What degrees do you hold and where were they earned?
A. A Ph.D. in sociology. at the University of Leipzig, a Ph.D. in anthropology from, the University of London.

Q. What is your field of special interest, Professor Manheim?
A. Social organization, juvenile delinquency and social theory.

Q. Have you published any articles in this particular field? Or any books?

Mr. Goodell: We don't want to interfere but we object to this if this is a repetition, simply cumulative of more expert opinion.

Mr. Greenberg: It is not, Your Honor.

Judge Huxman: What do you propose to rebut by the testimony of this witness? I take it you are qualifying him as an expert. Now just what testimony offered by the defendants are you proposing to rebut?

Mr. Greenberg: The clerk of the School Board stated that to the extent that there was a difference of library holdings between the colored and white schools, it was attributable to P. T. A. donations to the white schools. We intend to show that the maintenance of a segregated school system in Topeka has caused this difference in P. T. A. and community support of the colored as against the white schools.

Mr. Goodell: We object to that.

[fol. 344]   Mr. Greenberg: Directly rebuts——

Judge Huxman: Just a minute. The doctor isn't a resident of this community, is he?

In the hearing held by the District Court in the Kansas case, a NAACP attorney establishes the qualifications of an expert witness.

inferior beings and unworthy of the treatment accorded to whites.

The social scientists who testified also expressed doubt that white children with any degree of sensitivity could fail to be scarred by the practices of racial exclusion. Such children, they said, would tend to experience crippling feelings of guilt when struck by the realization that the creed of brotherly love that they had been taught to accept, and the practices of racial discrimination to which they had become accustomed, were mutually exclusive. But the expert testimony bore down much more heavily on the harmful effects of segregation on Negro children.

One of the most important witnesses for the Negroes was a noted psychologist, Kenneth B. Clark of City College in New York. In three of the school cases, Dr. Clark told about an experiment he had performed to measure the impact of segregation on Negro children. The experiment involved the use of two dolls, completely alike except that one was white and the other black. The children were asked to pick the doll that they found the most attractive, the one they would like to play with, the one they considered the prettiest. They were also asked to select the doll that looked "bad." And then, just to make sure that they were aware of racial differences, they would be asked which of the dolls was white and which was "colored." The Negro children who participated showed that they were fully aware of the difference between Negroes and whites, and that they emphatically preferred the white dolls.

The Pattern of Decision

The judges in the Topeka case were not unimpressed by the expert testimony. In the decision that they handed down, they held unanimously that compulsory segregation did indeed impair the development of Negro school children. But they declined to go beyond this conclusion to rule that educational segregation therefore constituted a violation of equal protection. As long as Negro and white elementary schools in

INDEX

In the index of their brief, the Negroes in the South Carolina case summarize the four principal points in their argument.

Topeka were substantially equal with respect to buildings, transportation, curricula, and educational qualification of teachers, they said, injunctive relief was not available.[12]

In the South Carolina case, in which Negroes sought to put an end to segregated schools in Clarendon County, the outcome was similar. Jim Crow education was the unbroken pattern in South Carolina, where the state constitution decreed that "no child of either race shall ever be permitted to attend a school provided for children of the other race." Throughout the state, separate schools for Negroes meant inferior schools, but in rural Clarendon County the situation was particularly deplorable. Classrooms were overcrowded and shabby; libraries and auditoriums were either nonexistent or grossly inadequate; and there was no nonsense about "frills" like lunchrooms or playgrounds.

The dismal record of Negro educational facilities in the South Carolina county was laid before the three-judge court that was convened in response to an application for a federal injunction. But just as in the Kansas case, the legal arguments made on behalf of the Negroes fell on deaf ears, with the judges declining to place segregated schooling outside the constitutional pale.[13] The court's opinion was written by John J. Parker, chief judge of the Fourth Circuit Court of Appeals, whose white supremacist views had long been a matter of public knowledge. As far back as 1930, when President Hoover had selected him for a seat on the Supreme Court, the Senate had refused to confirm the nomination after it was brought out, among other things, that the judge was against allowing Negroes to vote. No other nomination to the

[12] 98 F. Supp. 797 (1951). The citation refers to Vol. 98, p. 797 of the *Federal Supplement,* the compilation of decisions rendered by the District Courts (and also by the Court of Claims, which rules on financial claims against the government). Decisions of the Courts of Appeals, as well as those of the Court of Customs and Patent Appeals, are in the *Federal Reporter,* which is published in two consecutive series, cited as "F." and "F. 2d" respectively. Both the *Federal Reporter* and *Federal Supplement* are issued by a private company, the West Publishing Company.

[13] *Briggs* v. *Elliott,* 98 F. Supp. 529 (1951).

Supreme Court had been turned down by the Senate since 1874—and none has been rejected since.[14]

In the opinion that was filed by Judge Parker, one could not discern even a hint of dissatisfaction with the "separate but equal" doctrine. Instead, segregation was treated as a policy that any state legislature had the right to follow. Even insofar as equalizing physical facilities was concerned, the opinion showed no sense of urgency. Clarendon County was given six months to work on narrowing the gap between white and Negro schools, for by the end of that time significant improvement was expected as a result of a $75 million "school equalization" program that the state legislature had approved. The legislature had purposely appropriated the funds to cut the ground from under the plaintiffs in the case; the decision of the District Court proved that the strategy had been well chosen.

The South Carolina decision, however, was not unanimous. Judge J. Waties Waring wrote a stinging dissent denouncing the whole system of segregation as "unreasonable, unscientific, and based upon unadulterated prejudice." It reflected, he said, a "sadistic insistence of the 'white supremacists' in declaring that their will must be imposed irrespective of the rights of other citizens." These impassioned words were to cost their author dearly. The judge's stand prompted a violent reaction among his fellow South Carolinians, who had not quite recovered from another decision of his a few years earlier putting an end to the state's efforts to retain the "white primary." The jurist was subjected to a barrage of insults and abuse, and threats were even made against his life. Shortly thereafter he retired from the federal bench and moved out of the state.[15]

[14] Moreover, only five Supreme Court nominations in this century have aroused serious senatorial opposition. The Senate's influence on nominations, however, is greater than this statistic suggests, for Presidents are generally careful to clear a prospective nominee with key Senators before submitting his name formally.

[15] J. W. Peltason, *Fifty-eight Lonely Men: Southern Federal Judges and School Desegregation* (New York: Harcourt, Brace & World, 1961), p. 10.

But the Negroes did not have the support of even one judge in Virginia, where a three-judge court was convened to pass on school segregation in Prince Edward County. Since the state put several of its own social scientists on the stand to offer sanguine conclusions about the effects of segregation, the judges found it easy to ignore the expert witnesses on the other side. Segregation, they concluded, did "no hurt or harm to either race"; it was just "one of the ways of life in Virginia." Noting that Negro schools were being constructed rapidly, they found it necessary to do nothing more than express the hope that complete equalization of facilities would be accomplished "with all reasonable diligence and dispatch." [16]

The Difference in Delaware

Just as in Kansas and South Carolina, the defeat suffered by the Negroes in the Virginia case was at the hands of federal judges. Ironically, it was in the single school segregation suit lodged in a state court that the opponents of the "separate but equal" doctrine had their first taste of victory.

The state in which that victory came about was Delaware. Unlike the plaintiffs in Virginia, South Carolina, and Kansas, the Negroes in Delaware did not resort to a federal court, because they had no reason to anticipate that their own state judiciary would be hostile to their cause. Accordingly, they decided to seek relief in a state court. Since the judges of state courts are bound by oath to support the United States Constitution,[17] they, like federal judges, are able to issue injunctions prohibiting the enforcement of state laws that do violence to the Constitution. In Delaware, the issuance of injunctions is within the province of the Chancery Courts, which make up a separate branch of the state judicial system. The function of these courts is essentially preventive: to keep a wrongful

[16] Davis v. County School Board of Prince Edward County, 103 F. Supp. 337 (1952).
[17] Article VI, United States Constitution.

action from occurring rather than to assess damages against the perpetrator after the harm has been done. Under the principle of "equity," Chancery Courts are authorized to take action in advance where action after the fact would come too late to do the injured party any good. The preventive action may be an order to do something positive,[18] or it may be an injunction, which is essentially an order that something *not* be done. In this instance, it was an injunction against the enforcement of state laws requiring school segregation that Negro parents in Delaware were seeking on behalf of their children.[19]

The Delaware case was heard by Chancellor Collins J. Seitz.[20] After listening to extensive testimony from experts about the psychological effects of segregation, the chancellor rendered a decision that was in every respect a triumph for the Negro children of Newcastle County. Their segregated schools, he found, could not be compared to white schools in terms of criteria such as teacher-training, pupil-teacher ratio, extracurricular activities, physical plant, and the time and distance involved in travel. He ruled that under the circumstances the children would have to be admitted at once to the white schools, and to this end he issued an injunction that prohibited school officials from continuing to exclude them.

In taking this action, the Delaware chancellor parted company with the judges in the other states where Negro schools were found to be substantially inferior to white. Alone

[18] For example, the party to a contract may be compelled to fulfill the terms of the contract.

[19] Delaware is one of the few states that still maintain separate equity, or Chancery, courts. The more prevalent practice is for equitable jurisdiction to be vested in the ordinary statutory or common law courts, as is the case on the federal level, where the same tribunals function both as "courts of equity" and "courts of law."

[20] In Delaware, trials in Chancery Court are conducted by chancellors rather than judges. The title is British in origin. The Lord Chancellor, who was sometimes referred to as the "keeper of the King's conscience," was authorized as early as the fourteenth century to act for the Sovereign and grant relief as an act of grace when no effective remedy was available at common law. Chancellor Seitz, who heard the Delaware case, was appointed in 1966 to a judgeship on the United States Court of Appeals for the Third Circuit.

among them, he refrained from ordering or sanctioning an "equalization" program, and instead commanded immediate desegregation. Moreover, although he did not actually base his decision on this point, he went as far as to state that segregation in and of itself results in unfair treatment of Negro children, as it forces them to settle for "educational opportunities . . . substantially inferior to those available to white children otherwise similarly situated." [21]

Washington, D.C.

The fifth and last of the School Segregation Cases arose in the nation's capital, where a petition was filed in the Federal District Court on behalf of Negro children who had been turned away from a white public school solely because of their race. Although this suit had much in common with the others, the constitutional basis on which the Court was urged to act was entirely different. Instead of charging that segregated schools denied them "the equal protection of the laws," the Negroes in Washington claimed that they had been deprived of an aspect of their liberty "without due process of law."

This approach was necessary because of the peculiar federal status conferred on the capital city by the Constitution, which gives Congress exclusive legislative power "over such District . . . as may . . . become the Seat of the Government of the United States. . . ." [22] As a consequence of its federal standing, the government of the District of Columbia is not bound by those constitutional restrictions that apply only to the states. One such restriction is the Fourteenth Amendment.

[21] *Gebhart* v. *Belton,* 87 A. 2d 862 (1952). The "A. 2d." designation refers to recent volumes of the *Atlantic Reporter,* which publishes decisions of the state courts of Delaware and eight nearby states. Decisions of state courts elsewhere appear in other regional compilations included in the National Reporter System, a product of the West Publishing Company (the same company that publishes the *Federal Reporter* and the *Federal Supplement*).

[22] Article I, Section 8.

Since that Amendment had been designed to prevent states from continuing their previous mistreatment of Negroes, it had imposed no prohibitions whatever on the Federal Government, and it was of course the Federal Government that was responsible for the existence of segregated schools in the city of Washington.

But the District of Columbia is by no means exempt from all constitutional limitations. A number of the most significant limitations that do apply to federal instrumentalities are contained in the Bill of Rights, which was added to the original Constitution to prevent the newly created National Government from abusing its power and becoming an engine of tyranny. An important article of that Bill of Rights is the Fifth Amendment, which provides among other things that no person should "be deprived of life, liberty, or property, without due process of law . . ."

Although this due process clause on its face deals with procedure only, it was not long before the clause (and later its counterpart in the Fourteenth Amendment) was interpreted by the Supreme Court as possessing a substantive character as well. It was on the basis of due process that the Court began to strike down both congressional and state statutes regulating the economy when it found them to be arbitrary or not reasonably related to a legitimate object of legislation.[23]

Something akin to "substantive due process" was involved in the District of Columbia school case. Washington Negroes advanced the argument that their children were being deprived of the liberty to attend unsegregated schools, and that this was being done without due process of law since segregation bore no reasonable relationship to any proper governmental objective. The District Court in Washington, however, was not ready to accept such a radical proposition. It dismissed the complaint brought by the Negroes, declining even

[23] The Supreme Court's censorship of social welfare and economic legislation brought on a titanic struggle with President Franklin D. Roosevelt. After the struggle ended, with the Court capitulating to Roosevelt in 1937, the judicial practice of evaluating regulatory legislation in terms of substantive due process was abandoned.

to appoint a three-judge court to hear the case on its merits.

The proper tribunal before which such an action may be challenged is the Court of Appeals, and it was to it that the Negroes turned. But events later conspired to prevent the Court of Appeals from rendering a decision, for the Supreme Court wanted the District of Columbia case to be heard together with the other four school cases, which by that time it had agreed to review. Acting under a seldom-used rule that applies to cases "of such imperative public importance as to justify the deviation from normal appellate processes and to require immediate settlement in this Court," [24] the Justices invited the Negro litigants in the District of Columbia to petition for a Writ of Certiorari, which would bring their case from the Court of Appeals to the Supreme Court without further ado. The petition was of course filed at once, and it was promptly granted by the Supreme Court.

Intermediate Appeals

Thus the District of Columbia case did not receive appellate review at the intermediate level, going instead from the trial court directly to the Supreme Court. The same situation obtained in the Kansas, South Carolina, and Virginia cases; since the decisions had all been rendered by three-judge courts, they were all appealable right to the Supreme Court.

The only suit that *was* heard on Appeal before reaching the Supreme Court was the one from Delaware, which was in a class by itself since it had been handled from the start as a state case. On Appeal it went to the State Supreme Court, where a unanimous vote upheld the chancellor's ruling that the Negroes could no longer be excluded from the white schools. The decision rested on a narrow ground: the poor quality of the Negro schools. Not only did the State Supreme Court fail to question the constitutionality of segregation under more equitable circumstances; it also invited school au-

[24] Rule 20, *Rules of the Supreme Court*, 346 U.S. 968 (1954).

thorities to petition for a change in the order if they could
show at a later date that schools for Negroes were no longer
second class.[25]

Now that the State Supreme Court had acted, the Delaware case was ready for appeal to the United States Supreme
Court.[26]

Although this lawsuit alone received an appellate hearing
before reaching the Supreme Court, there were further proceedings in the South Carolina case, too. The proceedings
were held at the behest of the United States Supreme Court,
to which the decision of the three-judge District Court had
been appealed. What the Supreme Court did was to vacate
the judgment and return the case to the District Court. Its
purpose was to obtain a judicial assessment of the report that
had recently been filed by the county concerning progress
allegedly made in equalizing school facilities for Negroes and
whites.[27]

Per Curiam

The Supreme Court announced its action in the South
Carolina case in a short *per curiam* opinion rather than a full-
dress signed opinion. A *per curiam* is an opinion in which the
authorship is not attributed to any particular Justice. Such an
opinion is often handed down, as it was in the South Carolina

[25] *Gebhart* v. *Belton*, 91 A. 2d (1952). In the Court of Chancery,
the case had been designated *Belton* v. *Gebhart*, since Belton was the
plaintiff. It was the plaintiff, of course, who proved to be the winning
party, so the appeal to the State Supreme Court was taken by the other
side (Gebhart, the defendant in the courts below). The case then became *Gebhart* v. *Belton*, since the name of the party that is asking for
some judicial action normally comes first in the title of a case.

[26] An earlier appeal could not have been taken, since Congress has
limited the appellate jurisdiction of the Supreme Court to decisions
"rendered by the highest court of a state in which a decision could be
had." The purpose of the statutory limitation is to prevent the Supreme
Court from seizing jurisdiction in a case without waiting until the state
has completed its work.

[27] *Briggs* v. *Elliott*, 342 U.S. 350 (1952).

case, when the Court resolves a controversy summarily, without waiting for oral arguments or even briefs on the merits. Summary action is most common when the Court concludes that the question raised in a case has already been answered by previous—and usually recent—decisions.[28] In such instances, there may be nothing more in a *per curiam* opinion than a statement of the action agreed upon and citations of the case or cases considered controlling.

Increasingly, however, the Court has been handing down *per curiam* opinions in cases of great substantive significance, and when that happens it is not unusual for one or more of the Justices to note their dissent from a decision arrived at so peremptorily. That is precisely what took place when the Court issued its *per curiam* opinion in the South Carolina case. Two of the Justices, Hugo L. Black and William O. Douglas, could see no point in remanding the case to the District Court for an assessment of the progress made by Clarendon County in equalizing educational facilities. In a dissenting opinion that was announced together with the *per curiam,* they declared that additional information on the "equalization" program was "entirely irrelevant" to the constitutional question of whether segregation could be reconciled with the Fourteenth Amendment. The time was ripe, they said, for an immediate decision on that fundamental question.

But the other seven Justices did not agree, and the case went back to the District Court. After considering the steps taken by the county, that court concluded that substantial equality between the Negro and white school systems had been achieved or was in the process of being achieved. County officials, the court maintained, were trying to equalize facilities "as soon as humanly possible," and therefore "no good could be accomplished for anyone" through an order to end segregation.[29]

[28] Robert L. Stern and Eugene Gressman, *Supreme Court Practice,* 3rd ed. (Washington: Bureau of National Affairs, 1962), p. 186. In the 1964–65 term, 17 of the Supreme Court's 122 opinions were *per curiam.*

[29] This time the decision in the District Court was unanimous, for Judge Waring was no longer on the court. See p. 19.

This new decision by the District Court was promptly appealed to the Supreme Court. So were the other federal court decisions (from Kansas, Virginia, and the District of Columbia), as well as the decision of the State Supreme Court of Delaware.[30] The preliminaries had come to an end, and a momentous constitutional question was now on its way to the Supreme Court of the United States.

[30] The Delaware decision could be appealed to the Supreme Court because of a long-established principle that state judges do not necessarily have the last word when they act on federal questions. Otherwise, the same federal law could mean one thing in one state and something quite different in another, depending on what the supreme courts in each of the states *said* it meant. To prevent such conflict from taking place, the Supreme Court ruled in 1816 that it could constitutionally exercise the right to review state court interpretations of federal law, as Congress had provided almost three decades earlier in the Judiciary Act of 1789 (*Martin* v. *Hunter's Lessee*, 1 Wheaton 304 [1816]). The 1789 law was a comprehensive statute through which Congress created a system of federal trial courts and spelled out the jurisdiction of these courts as well as that of the Supreme Court.

3. The Strategy
of Litigation

It was no accident that five separate legal suits posing a single basic issue were on their way to the Supreme Court at approximately the same time. For although the various cases had been prosecuted in different courts and by different plaintiffs, a single organization was helping to direct them all. That organization was the nation's largest Negro rights group, the National Association for the Advancement of Colored People.

Since its founding in 1909, the NAACP had often selected the courtroom as the battlefield for its struggle on behalf of Negro rights. Its Legal Defense and Education Fund, dependent at first on volunteer lawyers, soon put together a full-time staff of its own to battle for such fundamental freedoms as the right to vote, and non-discriminatory treatment in southern courts. The lawyers on that staff became the envy of the American bar by winning one case after another in the federal courts. Within a few decades, the NAACP had more Supreme Court victories to its credit than any other organization of any kind, thus leading a Georgia senator to suspect that its director exercised "an almost occult power" over the Justices of the Supreme Court.[1]

The individual to whom this inadvertent compliment was

---

[1] Sen. Richard B. Russell (D., Ga.), quoted in Walter F. Murphy and C. Herman Pritchett, *Courts, Judges, and Politics: An Introduction to the Judicial Process* (New York: Random House, 1961), p. 275.

paid was Thurgood Marshall, who for many years was the director of the Legal Defense Fund.[2] As Marshall strode in triumph from courtroom to courtroom, his organization provided him with more money each year to carry on his work. In 1950, when the decision was made to challenge the Plessy doctrine head on, a budget of $150,000 was approved to finance litigation wherever conditions seemed most favorable for blazing new trails.[3]

Trail-blazing was what interested the NAACP the most. In the course of its development, the organization had decided to abandon the piecemeal approach of merely providing legal aid to the individual Negroes who were receiving unfair treatment at the hands of the law. Instead, it resolved to concentrate on challenging segregation where a victory in an individual case would also signify important progress for the whole group. In the words of a perceptive student of American race relations, the new policy of selecting cases "because of their general importance" meant that the NAACP had "shifted its emphasis from legal defense to legal offense." To this end, a "quite clearly conceived tactical plan" was followed by the organization.[4]

The attack on public school segregation was prepared with particular care. Never before had the NAACP legal arm acted more "like a strategy board of a field command, [paying] due regard to the manifold tactical and strategic problems that beset such a command."[5] This did not mean that the organization made any effort to stir up litigation for which it could then provide support. Local Negroes had enough home-

[2] Marshall was later appointed to a judgeship on the Federal Court of Appeals for the Second Circuit, and in 1965 he became Solicitor General of the United States.

[3] Alfred H. Kelly, "The School Desegregation Case," in John A. Garraty, ed., *Quarrels That Have Shaped the Constitution* (New York: Harper and Row, 1964), p. 251.

[4] Gunnar Myrdal, *An American Dilemma* (New York: McGraw-Hill, 1964), Vol. 2, p. 830. The first edition of the book was published in 1944.

[5] Henry J. Abraham, *The Judicial Process* (New York: Oxford University Press, 1962), p. 208.

grown complaints against their individual school boards to make such a tactic unnecessary. In Virginia, for example, students who had had enough walked out of a segregated school on their own, and the advice of NAACP lawyers was sought only afterward.[6] But here as elsewhere Marshall and his staff did their best to make sure that the issues would be framed in such a way as to pose a single fundamental issue: whether segregated public schools were forbidden by the Constitution.

Class Actions

In the cases for which it assumed responsibility, the NAACP made use of a device that is extremely useful in civil rights suits. Instead of having the individual plaintiffs seek judicial relief for themselves only, each case was framed as a "class action." Such an action may be brought by one or more members of a group that is simply too large for everyone in it to be made a party to a legal suit. When a judgment is rendered, it applies not only to those members of the "class" who are directly involved in the litigation, but to all others similarly situated.[7]

From the standpoint of the courts, "class action" suits make sense in terms of judicial economy, for one decision suffices to delineate the rights of a large number of persons who would otherwise have to file individual suits of their own. From the standpoint of an organization like the NAACP, the "class action" approach makes even better sense. The advantages have been described as follows:

> A single successful [suit] establishes the common right of all Negroes within a given jurisdiction to injunctive relief from a common discriminatory practice, eliminates the excessive cost of multiple litigation, permits individuals later to enforce the rights thus established by simple and speedy contempt actions,

[6] Shirley G. Powers, "The Thirteen-Year Filibuster," unpublished American University graduate paper, p. 15.

[7] "Class actions" are authorized by Rule 23 of the *Federal Rules of Civil Procedure for the United States District Courts*.

and prevents state officials from interminably delaying desegregation by continuing to discriminate against all who have not individually established a legal claim to relief.[8]

"Class actions" were also ideally suited to the NAACP's policy of working for adoption of broad legal principles that would change the face of America and not simply liberate one or two Negroes from discriminatory treatment. In employing the group approach, the NAACP was making a deliberate effort to affect public policy, using courts of law as an instrument for social change. Its hope was that the Negro could achieve in the courts what seemed completely unattainable in Congress, where so much power was in Southern hands.[9]

Of course the NAACP knew better than to try to influence the judicial process through the methods of direct pressure that are so prevalent in the halls of Congress. The tradition of a judiciary that is unapproachable to the point of aloofness is far too deeply ingrained for a prudent man to make any effort at buttonholing judges, and the life tenure enjoyed by members of the federal bench makes it more than a little difficult to threaten reprisals, in the accepted tradition of the congressional lobbyist. Although judges are sometimes the targets of concerted letter-writing campaigns, pressure-group activity in the courts is largely limited to providing legal and financial assistance in important test cases, with the effort also made at times to focus attention on a particular question through books, law review studies,[10] and articles in popular magazines.[11]

[8] Richard B. Wilson, "Massive Insistence or Massive Resistance? The Judicial Administration of the Civil Rights Revolution," *The George Washington Law Review*, Vol. 33 (April, 1965), p. 831.

[9] The virtual veto power that has been held by the South over civil rights legislation is described by this author in *A Bill Becomes a Law: Congress Enacts Civil Rights Legislation* (New York: Macmillan, 1966).

[10] One Justice of the Supreme Court has proposed that law reviews list any "relevant affiliations" of their contributors, and wherever applicable note the fact that an article was written for a fee paid by a special interest group. William O. Douglas, "Law Reviews and Full Disclosure," *Washington Law Review*, Vol. 40 (June, 1965), p. 232.

[11] For a study of pressure groups in the judicial process, see Clement E. Vose, "Litigation as a Form of Pressure Group Activity," *Annals of the American Academy of Political and Social Science*, Vol. 319 (September, 1958), p. 20.

For the School Segregation Cases, the NAACP marshaled all of its resources. At least in a certain sense, almost two decades of planning went into the litigation, for the NAACP lawyers regarded their earlier attacks on segregated graduate and professional schools as an effort to gain a beachhead for the ultimate assault on segregated elementary schools.

Strategic Planning

The lawyer who now directs the NAACP's Legal Defense and Education Fund has explained why his organization began with higher education instead of giving priority to elementary education. For one thing, "inequality in higher education could be proved with [greater] ease [since] there were virtually no public Negro graduate and professional schools in the South, and judges would readily understand the shortcomings of separate legal education, which some of the cases concerned. [Moreover,] since it would be financially impossible to furnish true equality—both tangible and intangible—desegregation would be the only practicable way to fulfill the constitutional obligation of equal protection" for students in graduate and professional schools.[12] The policy of starting at the college level seemed wise to the NAACP strategists from still another angle. Their assessment of Southern white psychology had convinced them that resistance to integration at that level would be far less determined than with respect to elementary schools.[13]

[12] The NAACP lawyer mentions two other factors: "Small numbers of mature students were involved, undercutting opposing arguments based on violence and widespread social revolution. Finally, Negro leadership would be augmented whether there was desegregation or enriched separate schools." Jack Greenberg, *Race Relations and American Law* (New York: Columbia University Press, 1959), p. 37.

[13] Thurgood Marshall thought he detected something of a paradox in the relative equanimity with which the South contemplated the possibility that graduate and professional schools would be integrated. "Those racial supremacy boys somehow think," he said, "that little kids of six or seven are going to get funny ideas about sex and marriage just from going to school together, but for some equally funny reasons youngsters in law school aren't supposed to feel that way." He added: "We didn't

For all these reasons, the NAACP postponed action on primary and secondary schools until the principle of segregated education had been chipped away through significant victories in institutions of higher education. Only when that had been accomplished did they venture to take the next step.

Certiorari

In their effort to persuade the Supreme Court to accept the five public school cases for review, the NAACP lawyers invoked two separate and distinct procedures. For the cases originating in Delaware and the District of Columbia, they filed petitions for Writs of Certiorari; they asked the Supreme Court to hear the other three cases "on Appeal."

Certiorari is the more commonly used channel through which cases are carried to the Supreme Court. In Petitioning for Certiorari, a litigant who has lost a case in a lower court asks the Supreme Court to set the stage for reviewing the judgment by announcing that it wishes the record of the case in the court below "to be certified" and submitted to it. Whether the Supreme Court will do so or not is completely within its discretion.

The present Certiorari procedure dates back only to 1925. Before that time, the Supreme Court had no general power to sift the cases it was asked to review and to reject those that did not merit a hearing at so high a level. Under the permissive rules that Congress had devised, 80 percent of the Supreme Court's cases were appealed to it as a matter of right, and thus a multitude of comparatively inconsequential legal controversies were forced on it for decision. So easy was it for litigants to carry their appeals all the way to the top that almost constantly there was a formidable backlog of cases in the Supreme Court.

---

get it but we decided that if that was what the South believed, then the best thing for the moment was to go along." Quoted in Kelly, *op. cit.*, p. 254.

When William Howard Taft became Chief Justice in 1921, he set out to improve this state of affairs, designating three of his colleagues as a special committee responsible for drafting legislation to help relieve congestion in the Supreme Court.[14] The bill that the committee came up with met with Taft's enthusiastic approval. But congressional action was required before it could go into effect, since it is the Legislative Branch and not the Court itself that establishes the ground rules under which the Judiciary operates.

The so-called Judges' Bill was introduced in the House and Senate in 1922 by members of Congress friendly with Taft. In an effort to insure that the bill would be enacted into law, the Chief Justice shed his judicial robes and began to act for all the world like a high-powered lobbyist. Assuming personal charge of the campaign to see the bill through, he testified before congressional committees, delivered a series of public addresses, and even went so far as to bombard key members of Congress with correspondence. And that was not all. A student of the judicial process relates that Taft also

> worked closely with the chief lobbyist for the American Bar Association as well as with the Attorney General and the Solicitor General of the United States. . . . When legislators appeared uninterested in the Court's proposal, [he] took to patrolling the halls of Congress, buttonholing influential solons and cajoling them into supporting his measure. . . . Through his old friend Attorney General Harry Daugherty, [he] even persuaded Coolidge to allow him to draft a few paragraphs strongly supporting adoption of the Judges' Bill for the President's annual message to Congress.[15]

The unprecedented lobbying effort was crowned with success, and in 1925 the Judges' Bill was approved by both Houses of Congress and signed into law.

---

[14] The Justices whom Taft selected in 1921 were William Rufus Day, James C. McReynolds, and Willis Van Devanter. In the following year, when Justice Day retired from the Court, the Chief Justice named George Sutherland to the committee.

[15] Walter F. Murphy, *Wiretapping on Trial: A Case Study in the Judicial Process* (New York: Random House, 1965), pp. 53–54.

Sifting and Winnowing

Probably the most important reform instituted by the 1925 statute was a new Certiorari procedure, enabling the Justices to pick and choose among the ordinary cases they were asked to review. The Supreme Court, for the first time in its history, now had complete control of its docket.

The Court itself soon decided that it would not be necessary for a majority of the Justices to vote for Certiorari in order to accept a case. Under an informal agreement still in effect, they concluded that the consent of any four of the nine would be sufficient. Nevertheless, only a small fraction of the petitions for Certiorari—not much more than 10 percent—are normally successful. Partly this is so because there is a natural limit to the amount of work that nine men can do. But a more substantive consideration is also involved: the belief that it is not the Court's proper function to try to rectify every injustice and correct every error committed anywhere in the Federal and state judicial systems. Accordingly, cases in which the outcome is important only to the parties themselves are rejected, and the Court conserves its time and energy for those which, as Chief Justice Vinson once put it, "present questions whose resolution will have immediate importance far beyond the particular facts and parties involved." [16]

But what about the disappointed litigant who is convinced that a case important to him has been wrongly decided? Should it be so difficult for him to obtain access to the Supreme Court? The classic reply was provided by Taft in a statement he prepared for a congressional committee:

> No litigant is entitled to more than two chances—namely to the original trial and to a review—and the intermediate courts of review are provided for that purpose. When a case goes beyond that, it is not primarily to preserve the rights of

[16] Quoted in Glendon A. Schubert, *Constitutional Politics* (New York: Holt, Rinehart & Winston, 1960), p. 92.

the litigants. The Supreme Court's function is for the purpose of expounding and stabilizing principles of law for the benefit of the people of the country, [and] passing upon constitutional questions and other important questions of law for the public benefit.[17]

Since the Court subscribes to this view of its legitimate role, a well-drawn petition for Certiorari does not concentrate unduly on proving that a case has been decided incorrectly in a lower court. Instead, the petition attempts to persuade the Justices that the case poses fundamental issues which cry out for resolution by the highest court in the land. The Justices will probably be sympathetic if, for example, the Federal Court of Appeals that decided the case interpreted a particular statute differently than another Court of Appeals. And a receptive attitude may also be expected if it can be shown either that a Federal Court of Appeals "has so far departed from the accepted and usual course of judicial proceedings . . . as to call for an exercise of this court's power of supervision," or that a state or federal court has decided an important question of federal law.[18]

A most important question of federal law—constitutional law, at that—was involved in the School Segregation Cases, and it was on this basis that the Supreme Court was asked to grant Certiorari to review the decisions involving Delaware and the District of Columbia. In each of these two cases, the NAACP attorneys filed copies of their petitions with the Clerk of the Court, whose office is the principal communications link between the Justices on the one hand and litigants and their lawyers on the other. The Clerk's Office did not circulate the petitions to the Justices immediately, however, for the parties on the other side had thirty days in which to submit their "briefs in opposition." Not until then were the NAACP petitions, together with the reply briefs, distributed to the individual Justices.

[17] Hearings before the Committee on the Judiciary of the House of Representatives on H.R. 10479, 67th Cong., 2d Sess., p. 2.
[18] Rule 19, *Rules of the Supreme Court*, 346 U.S. 967–68 (1954).

Appeal

In the other three cases—those from Kansas, South Carolina, and Virginia—it was not necessary for the lawyers who represented the Negroes to resort to petitions for Certiorari. Another method, known simply as Appeal, was used to request Supreme Court review. The Appeal procedure may be employed only when a case fits into one of the categories that Congress has held deserving of Supreme Court review as a matter of right. Most of the cases to which Congress has given this privileged status—only a small percentage of the Court's total load—involve one of two questions: whether a particular law, either federal or state, violates the United States Constitution; or whether a state law that is under fire conflicts with a valid federal law and must therefore fall, in accordance with the supremacy clause of the United States Constitution.[19] If, for example, a federal law has been declared unconstitutional by a state court, or if a state law has been declared unconstitutional by a federal court, Appeal is available in order to bring the case before the Supreme Court. The same holds true when a State Supreme Court declines to invalidate a state law in the face of a substantial contention that the law violates either a federal statute or a provision of the Constitution. And Appeal is also the proper method for obtaining review of any decision by a three-judge Federal District Court on whether to issue an injunction against the enforcement of either a state law or an Act of Congress.

Although the Appeal procedure was intended by Congress to make access to the Supreme Court in certain instances a right rather than a privilege, a wide gulf exists between the

[19] Section 2 of Article VI contains the following wording: "This Constitution, and the Laws of the United States which shall be made in Pursuance thereof; and all Treaties made . . . under the Authority of the United States, shall be the supreme Law of the Land; and the Judges in every State shall be bound thereby, any Thing in the Constitution or Laws of any State to the Contrary notwithstanding."

legislative intent and the way things work in practice. The reason is that the members of the Court found, not long after the Judges' Bill was enacted,[20] that far more cases were being presented to them on Appeal than they could possibly handle. In an effort to improve the situation, they came up with an ingenious new formula requiring the submission of a preliminary Jurisdictional Statement by a party that wanted to bring up a case on Appeal. The Jurisdictional Statement could then be treated much the same as a petition for a Writ of Certiorari, with the approval of at least four members of the Court required for acceptance. Otherwise, without briefs or oral argument, the Appeal would be dismissed, and the Court would announce that the Jurisdictional Statement had either failed to present a "substantial federal question" or else had not proved that the Court really had jurisdiction to decide the case on its merits.

Without any doubt, the new practice introduced almost as strong an element of discretion in Appeals as in Certiorari cases. In a typical year the Court actually refuses to entertain approximately half of the cases brought to it on Appeal. Practically speaking, therefore, Certiorari cases and Appeal cases are still distinct from each other, but it is a distinction without a significant difference.[21]

---

[20] The Judges' Bill introduced the Appeal device as well as the present Certiorari procedure.

[21] Yet, when the Justices decide not to hear a case brought to them on Appeal from a three-judge federal court, they recognize that a peremptory dismissal would mean that there had been no appellate review whatever of the trial court's decision. Therefore, instead of dismissing such cases, they profess to consider them "on the merits." Usually, however, this consideration is more fiction than fact, for the lower court's decision is affirmed summarily. What the Court does technically is to note probable jurisdiction, and at the same time affirm the decision being appealed, though neither full-dress briefs have been filed nor oral argument held. Glendon A. Schubert, *Judicial Policy-Making: The Political Role of the Courts* (Chicago: Scott, Foresman, 1965), p. 72.

The Meaning of a Denial

The Supreme Court, in firm control of its docket, elects to hear no more than perhaps 160 cases of the 3,000 or so that it is urged to accept each year. In the remaining cases, the decision of the lower court is allowed to stand. The Justices never tire of explaining that their refusal to take a case does not in any way signify that they agree with what the lower court has done. Suspicion persists, however, that they do tend to reject the cases in which they are satisfied that a correct decision has been rendered. Two students of the court observed that during a three-year period the judgments of lower courts were reversed by the Supreme Court in nearly two-thirds of the cases accepted for review. From this fact the inference was drawn that at the screening stage the Justices *had* apparently been influenced by whether they agreed with the decisions of the lower courts, and had not acted solely on the basis of whether the issues presented were important enough to merit review. The authors of the article put it this way: "Since the grants of Certiorari came most often in cases where the Court disapproved of the decisions below, the denial of Certiorari may imply at least some degree of approval of the decision below. . . ." [22]

Whether or not this conclusion is sound, it cannot be denied that, for the parties directly involved in a case, refusal by the Supreme Court to grant review is indeed tantamount to approval of the lower court's action. Since the Court, at least in a certain sense, is thus making a decision while ostensibly refusing to make a decision, its disposition of Certiorari petitions and Jurisdictional Statements ranks among its most important actions.

It is only fitting, therefore, that the sifting of new cases is

[22] Fowler V. Harper and George C. Pratt, "What the Supreme Court Did Not Do During the 1951 Term," *University of Pennsylvania Law Review*, Vol. 101 (1953), p. 439.

not done in a casual manner. There is no disposition, for example, to delegate the screening responsibility to individual Justices or even to panels. Decisions at this stage, as at every other stage, are made by the full Court.

Law Clerks

The litigant who carries his case to the Supreme Court is required to file no fewer than forty copies of his petition or Jurisdictional Statement with the Clerk of the Court.[23] All members of the Court receive copies, together with copies of any response submitted by the other side. At this stage, Justices do not customarily confer with each other on the question of whether the case should be heard.[24] They do, however, work closely with the law clerks on their staffs.

Clerks are usually recent law school graduates, almost always at the top of their class, who serve in the Supreme Court under an internship arrangement. Each Associate Justice is entitled to two clerks, whereas the Chief Justice is allowed three. It is up to the individual member of the Court to arrange for the selection of his own clerks; a fairly general practice is to delegate the responsibility to friends who teach at leading law schools.[25]

The Justices use their law clerks for a wide variety of chores. Research assistance is the most common type of service rendered, but some members of the Court also make a practice

[23] The only exception is made for cases that are brought by individuals who cannot afford the expense of pursuing their appeal in the regular way. Such indigent plaintiffs may file only a single copy of their petition and still have their case brought to the attention of the court. The subject of in forma pauperis appeals is discussed on pp. 47–49.

[24] William J. Brennan, Jr., "Inside View of the High Court," The New York Times Magazine, October 6, 1963, p. 100.

[25] Some law clerks have later gone on to illustrious careers. For example, Dean G. Acheson, who clerked for Justice Louis D. Brandeis, became Secretary of State, and Francis Biddle, who worked for Justice Oliver Wendell Holmes, was later appointed Attorney General. So far, only one former clerk has been named to a seat on the Supreme Court: Byron White, who served on the staff of Chief Justice Vinson.

of trying out fresh ideas on their clerks. Even when a clerk is permitted to draft an opinion, he may very well not recognize much of his work after the Justice gets through "editing," for in most instances the members of the Court do a great deal of their own writing. In this respect, they are quite unlike officials of the Legislative and Executive Branches, who depend heavily on staff assistance.[26]

Even though the law clerks do not always get to do much opinion writing, they do play a significant role in the screening of Certiorari petitions. A former clerk to Justice Robert H. Jackson once described the process as he had participated in it:

> In Justice Jackson's office, the petitions for Certiorari which were scheduled to be discussed at the next conference of the Justices were split between the two clerks. Each clerk would then prepare memoranda on the petitions assigned to him. These would include the facts of the case, the law as declared by the lower court, and a brief summary of previous cases involving the same points. They concluded with a recommendation by the clerk either that the petition be granted or that it be denied.

Although the same observer thought that the clerks had too much influence on the disposition of Certiorari petitions,[27] he admitted that the Justice whom he had served did not rely exclusively on the memoranda prepared by the clerks and would himself "study the petitions in order to determine his vote."[28]

[26] There are, of course, exceptions. Clerks in the office of Chief Justice Vinson, for example, were regularly used as "ghosts." An assistant to one of Vinson's colleagues spoke of how the Chief Justice "is said to have done all his 'writing' with his hands in his pockets, outlining to his clerks generally what he wanted, and then criticizing this bit or that in a clerk's draft and making suggestions for revision." John P. Frank, *Marble Palace: The Supreme Court in American Life* (New York: Knopf, 1958), p. 118.

[27] He hinted darkly that the influence of the clerks tended to push the disposition of Certiorari petitions in a leftward direction.

[28] William H. Rehnquist, "Who Writes Decisions of the Supreme Court?" *U. S. News and World Report,* December 13, 1957, pp. 74–75. Jackson himself was amused that some people thought that the clerks

In Conference

An expeditious procedure has been devised for handling those Certiorari petitions which do not persuade even a single Justice that Supreme Court review is merited. In the 1930's, Chief Justice Charles Evans Hughes instituted the practice of circulating among his colleagues a "black list" of cases on which he could see no reason at all for further action. Except when one of the Associate Justices expressed disagreement—and such instances were few and far between—the Court would announce without further ado that the petitions had been denied.[29] Every Chief Justice since Hughes' time has continued the practice in order to avoid wasting precious conference time on cases devoid of any merit.[30]

Certiorari petitions that have not been consigned to oblivion through the "unanimous consent" procedure, and also the Jurisdictional Statements that have been filed in cases on Appeal, are taken up by the Justices at one of their regular conferences, usually held weekly when the Court is sitting. Such a conference was held on June 7, 1952.

Five minutes before ten o'clock that Saturday morning, a buzzer sounded in the chambers of the Justices to summon them to the conference room. Upon entering, each man shook hands with every one of his colleagues before taking his seat at the large rectangular table in the middle of the room.[31]

"constitute a kind of junior court which decides the fate of certiorari petitions." He suggested impishly that perhaps "the Senate no longer need bother about confirmation of Justices but ought to confirm the appointment of law clerks." Quoted by Justice Tom Clark, "Internal Operation of the United States Supreme Court," *Journal of the American Judicature Society*, Vol. 43 (August, 1959), p. 48.

[29] Merlo J. Pusey, *Charles Evans Hughes* (New York: Columbia University Press, 1963), Vol. II, p. 672.

[30] Most of the cases screened out by the unanimous consent procedure are on the Miscellaneous Docket (discussed on pp. 47–49).

[31] The hand-shaking ceremony is observed whenever the Justices assemble for a conference or a public session. A member of the Court once remarked that the ceremony, when held before a conference, made

Chief Justice Vinson and the Senior Associate Justice, Hugo L. Black, sat at opposite ends of the table, with four of the other Associate Justices to the left of the Chief Justice, and the remaining three to his right. The room was panelled in oak, with lawbooks from floor to ceiling on one side. A portrait of John Marshall hung above the mantle of a marble fireplace. Each Justice had in front of him a "conference list" noting the cases that were ready for disposition and some had already indicated on it their preliminary preferences for action that should be taken.

On this day, as always, the atmosphere of the conference was sober and serious.[32] Aside from the nine Justices, no one was permitted to be present—not secretaries, law clerks, nor even pages—for Supreme Court conferences are a rare oasis of privacy and confidentiality in a capital where there are few secrets.

Ever since 1857 the Court has gone to great lengths to preserve the security of its conference proceedings. In that year one of the Justices, John Catron, evidently told President-elect James Buchanan how *Dred Scott* v. *Sandford,* perhaps the most sensitive case of the century, was going to be decided, and Buchanan made use of the advance information in his Inaugural Address. Determined that this kind of episode should never be repeated, the Justices have made a virtual fetish of secrecy from that time on. Not only are they themselves careful never to let a word drop to outsiders about any case that is up for decision, but they also try hard to guard against the possibility of leaks by employees of the Court. Thus even when something unforeseen arises while they are

---

him think of a boxing ring with the referee saying, "Shake hands, go to your corner and come out fighting." James F. Byrnes, quoted in Alan F. Westin, *An Autobiography of the Supreme Court: Off-the-Bench Commentary by the Justices* (New York: Macmillan, 1963), p. 154.

[32] Time was when conferences were more spirited affairs. John Marshall allowed wine to be served on rainy days, and—as legend has it—"if the sun was shining, [he] would order wine anyway, since 'our jurisdiction is so vast that it must be raining somewhere.'" The Foundation of the Federal Bar Association, *Equal Justice Under Law: The Supreme Court in American Life* (Washington, 1965), p. 29.

deliberating and it becomes necessary for a secretary to deliver a note to one of them, the rule against admitting anyone else to the conference room is not suspended. Instead, the secretary knocks at the door and the junior Justice leaves the room to get the message. In 1952, Justice Sherman Minton, appointed to the Court by President Truman only three years earlier, had the least seniority among his colleagues and was therefore, as some phrased it, "the best-paid messenger in Washington."

Nine Men

Chief Justice Vinson, who presided at the conference when the School Segregation Cases were first considered, was another Truman appointee. Although he, like Minton, was a Democrat and the appointee of a Democratic President, the reputation he had earned was that of a conservative, generally showing scant sympathy for individuals who claimed that their civil liberties had been infringed by some agency of the Government. Segregation questions, however, seemed to be in a special category for him. It was Vinson who had written the opinion merely two years earlier ordering the admission of a Negro applicant to an all-white law school on the ground that the segregated institution provided by the state was inferior in terms of the intangible factors "that make for greatness in a law school." [33]

Vinson and Minton were not the sole Truman appointees on the 1952 Court. There were also Tom Clark of Texas and Harold H. Burton of Ohio. Clark had been a Democratic Attorney General and Burton a Republican Senator. Like Truman's other appointees, however, they were equally conservative on civil liberties questions.

The five remaining Associate Justices were all Democrats who had been named to the Court by President Franklin D. Roosevelt, but their records by no means indicated that they shared a common judicial philosophy. No two men could have

[33] *Sweatt* v. *Painter,* 339 U.S. 629 (1950).

been further apart, as a matter of fact, than Hugo Black and Felix Frankfurter. Black, who was Roosevelt's first appointee to the Supreme Court, had once been a member of the Ku Klux Klan, but he was a staunch foe of racism and his actions as a Justice were those of an uncompromising libertarian. Frankfurter, too, had views on segregation that were impeccably liberal, but he never ceased explaining that a judge's private philosophy should have no bearing at all on his official actions. He was an ardent advocate of what he liked to call "judicial restraint," which in practice often meant acquiescing in governmental abridgments of individual liberty.

The other three Rooseveltians on the Vinson Court were Justice Douglas, whose position was close to Black's; Justice Jackson, who was often allied with Frankfurter; and Stanley F. Reed, who, like the Chief Justice, was a conservative on questions of civil liberties.

But such characterizations are crude at best, and, like many a Supreme Court, the Justices who took their places in the conference room to begin consideration of the School Segregation Cases were hard to label and impossible to predict.

The Chief Justice

Presiding over the conference in June 1952 was Chief Justice Vinson. The formal powers and prerogatives of a Chief Justice have always been minimal; [34] perhaps the only one of any consequence today is his right to determine in every case—except when he finds himself on the minority side—which of his colleagues will write the "opinion of the Court" explaining the basis for the decision that has been reached. [35] Even his salary is a trifling five hundred dollars more than that

[34] Among these is the power to fill certain staff positions. For instance, the Chief Justice appoints the Clerk, Librarian, and Marshal of the Court, as well as the Director of the Administrative Office of the United States Courts.

[35] This process is explained on pp. 103–05.

of his colleagues: $40,000 as compared to $39,500 for the Associate Justices. It would seem as though Congress wants to emphasize that the Chief Justice, though often described as *primus inter pares,* is in reality more the equal of his fellow Justices than the first among them.[36]

But the prestige conferred by the office of Chief Justice is immense, and a man who possesses both determination and tact can exercise an enduring influence on the course of American law.[37] Certainly no one today would relinquish the position to run for a governorship, as did John Jay, the first Chief Justice, and it is highly unlikely that anyone would decline the office, as Patrick Henry did.

When Chief Justice Vinson opened the conference on June 7, 1952, there was one item of business that had to be disposed of before the segregation issue could be discussed. The following Monday would be a "decision day," and the Justices had to ascertain which opinions would be ready for announcement at that time. Not until that had been done

---

[36] Although his salary is hardly any higher than theirs, the Chief Justice does enjoy certain perquisites denied to the other members of the Court. He is provided, for instance, with a chauffeur-driven limousine, and he is also entitled to an extra secretary and a third law clerk. The additional staff assistance is not really a luxury, however. The secretary is needed because of the heavy burden of administrative responsibilities that the Chief Justice must shoulder (particularly as chairman of the Judicial Conference of the United States and in connection with the work of the Administrative Office of the United States Courts). And the extra law clerk helps with the flood of *in forma pauperis* petitions.

[37] Justice Frankfurter once made an effort to explain the subtleties of the process:

> It isn't what he says in his opinions that is more important than what his brethren say, but what he advises on the mechanics of doing the job—should we give a lawyer extra time, should we hear this case now or later, should we grant a rehearing if the Court is divided; things that pertain to the way that the business should be done, things that cannot properly be managed without knowledge of the nature of the business, or, since you deal with eight other human beings, without knowledge of the ways of the other eight Justices.

Felix Frankfurter, "Chief Justices I Have Known," *Virginia Law Review,* Vol. 39 (1953), p. 894.

could they turn their attention to the more recent cases brought before them through Appeal and Certiorari.

At this stage, only the School Segregation Cases from Kansas and South Carolina were on the conference list; the other three were still in the lower courts. Only four affirmative votes were required to accept the two cases for briefing, oral argument, and a decision on the merits.[38] Exactly that many were in fact cast,[39] and thus the first major hurdle for the Kansas and South Carolina cases was surmounted.

Although the Justices had no more cases to deal with that day on the issue of segregation, their conference was not yet over. There were additional Jurisdictional Statements to take care of, plus a large number of Certiorari petitions. According to established procedure, the petitions were taken up in a prescribed order. First came those on the Appellate Docket, and then the ones on the Miscellaneous Docket. The Appellate Docket contains cases brought to the Court by litigants who can afford the $100 docketing fee on top of the costs of printing necessary documents. For cases brought by indigents, the Miscellaneous Docket is maintained.

"In Forma Pauperis"

A petitioner need not be completely destitute to take advantage of the procedure available to indigents; it is open to anyone who would be rendered destitute by the costs of a normal Appeal. Although an affidavit must be filed certifying that he is unable to pay the costs, the Court shows no inclination to check the veracity of this sworn statement. Thus any petitioner who submits the affidavit is permitted to prosecute

[38] The conference usually takes no formal votes except in particularly complicated cases, when discussion alone may not sufficiently clarify the exact position of each Justice. (From interview with Justice John Marshall Harlan, January 12, 1966.)

[39] The traditional docket book used by Chief Justices for recording votes is obviously not of recent vintage. Justice Clark says that its appearance indicates it has been "handed down to us by the first of the Justices." Clark, *op. cit.*, p. 50.

his case *in forma pauperis,* which means the documents per-
taining to his case need not be printed, or even typewritten, if
that is not possible.[40] In some instances, petitions written out
in pencil on scraps of writing paper have been received and
accepted.

About 1,500 cases are brought to the Supreme Court each
year *in forma pauperis,* most of them from men in prison;
the number actually exceeds those in which the fees have been
paid. Although some petitions are nearly indecipherable and
many do not even purport to be in the proper legal form, every
one is carefully scrutinized. In each case, one of the Chief
Justice's law clerks prepares an explanatory memorandum that
is then circulated among all the members of the Court.[41] The
petition itself makes the rounds only in capital cases or if
one of the Justices asks to see it. Moreover, the party that has
custody of the petitioner does not always see fit to file a
response. Although the United States Government invariably
submits an answer when a federal prisoner petitions the Court,
only a few of the states follow the same policy. In approximately half of the remaining state cases, the Chief Justice re-
quests a response, indicating by this action that at least in his
view a substantial question has been raised in the petition.

In a typical year, the overwhelming majority of Miscellaneous cases—as many as 97 percent—are found to be
unmeritorious. No doubt the Court would not be saddled with
so many frivolous *in forma pauperis* petitions if counsel were
available to the inmates who file them, for a lawyer would be
in a position to weed out those without any chance of success
at all. Even more importantly, a lawyer could help see to it
that petitions which did deserve to be filed were properly
prepared.[42]

[40] Rule 53, *Rules of the Supreme Court,* 346 U.S. 1003 (1954).
[41] The law clerks assigned to the other Justices may help screen
petitions when the Chief Justice's clerks find themselves overburdened.
[42] A member of the Supreme Court has gone so far as to label the
unavailability of counsel at the petitioning stage "a blot on the legal
profession." Tom Clark, Address to University of Minnesota Law School
Alumni Association, April 13, 1959.

In spite of the shortcomings of the present system, some Miscellaneous petitions nevertheless do raise critical questions of criminal law, and principles of great significance may be established when these questions are resolved in favor of the petitioner. A celebrated example was the 1963 case in which the Court established for the first time the rule that no conviction could stand if the defendant had not enjoyed the assistance of counsel at his trial.[43]

When the Court grants an *in forma pauperis* petition, the case is transferred from the special Miscellaneous Docket to the regular Appellate Docket and an attorney is appointed to represent the indigent. The attorney may be a former Supreme Court law clerk, or a law professor, or a practitioner whom the Justices themselves know personally or by reputation. Invariably he is a distinguished member of the bar and an expert in criminal law. In the 1963 case establishing the right to counsel in state trials, for example, the attorney who was chosen to argue the case was Abe Fortas, later to be named a Supreme Court Justice. An appointed counsel serves without pay; not even his expenses (except for a single round-trip ticket to Washington) are defrayed.

Official Announcement

In their conference on June 7, 1952, the Justices went through the cases on the Miscellaneous Docket and then adjourned.[44] Nothing they had done at the conference could

[43] *Gideon* v. *Wainwright*, 372 U.S. 335 (1963). Previously, counsel had been required in state trials only for capital cases and where special circumstances were present that made for unfairness. *Betts* v. *Brady*, 316 U.S. 455 (1942). The story of the Gideon case is told in Anthony Lewis, *Gideon's Trumpet* (New York: Random House, 1964).

[44] Because the summer recess was about to begin, the disposition of *in forma pauperis* petitions was the final item on the conference agenda. There were no recently argued cases to be voted on, for the Court had, according to custom, held its last oral arguments in early spring in order to leave enough time for deciding the cases and preparing written opinions before the end of the term.

compare in importance, of course, to their decision to hear the two School Segregation Cases in the fall.

On the following Monday, the official announcement was made that the cases from Kansas and South Carolina had been accepted by the Court. Such an announcement is not made orally; rather, it is made by posting notices in the Court building, by dispatching telegrams to the various lawyers,[45] and by making the information available to the press. In this manner, the news was released that Probable Jurisdiction had been noted in *Brown* v. *Board of Education* and *Briggs* v. *Elliot,* the Kansas and South Carolina cases, respectively, and that oral argument had been set for the week of October 13, 1952.[46]

The announcement came on the last day of the 1951–1952 term of Court, right before a three-month summer recess. By the time the Justices reconvened in October, the school case from Virginia had come to them on Appeal, and in one of their first conferences of the new term [47] they voted to hear that case, too.

Since there was, as the Court expressed it, a "similarity" between the Virginia case and the two cases (from Kansas and South Carolina) that had previously been accepted for review, all three suits were consolidated and scheduled to be argued consecutively. Moreover, the Court took note of the fact that a fourth school case was pending in the Court of Appeals for

[45] After the Court decides whether to accept a case, the Clerk's Office notifies counsel for each side at once. The notification is made by letter unless the lawyer has requested that a collect telegram be sent.

[46] It is not customary for the Court to announce how the different Justices have voted on Appeals and Certiorari petitions, although individual members may state their positions if they like. Justice Frankfurter had a roundabout method for disclosing his vote when the Court denied a petition that he had wanted to grant. He would write a little essay explaining that a denial of Certiorari by no means necessarily signified agreement with the court below. Other Justices employ no such circumlocution, preferring to note plainly their disagreement with what has been done.

[47] At the beginning of the term in October, conferences are held daily in order to dispose of the mountain of Appeals and Certiorari petitions that have piled up during the summer.

the District of Columbia, and concluded that it would be desirable to hear that case, too, along with the others. It therefore invited the Negro litigants in the District of Columbia case to file a petition for Certiorari, even though the lower court had not yet acted.

The grouping of the four suits meant that oral argument on Kansas and South Carolina, scheduled to take place within a week, had to be postponed in order to allow enough time for briefs to be filed in the two new cases. Accordingly, the Court announced that the argument would be put off until December. Justice Douglas, impatient to begin work on the segregation cases, noted his dissent.[48]

The Negro litigants in the District of Columbia case were quick to accept the invitation to file for Certiorari, and their petition was granted on November 10th. By then the Delaware case had also completed its journey through the lower courts, and it was promptly consolidated with the others. Hence there would be five School Segregation Cases to be argued before the Supreme Court of the United States.

[48] *Brown v. Board of Education*, 344 U.S. 1 (1952).

4. Friends of the Court

Of the five School Segregation Cases scheduled for oral argument, the one from Kansas had been the first to reach the Supreme Court. For this reason, the four suits challenging the imposition of school segregation by a state were grouped under the single title, *Brown* v. *Board of Education of Topeka.* Since the remaining case—the one from the District of Columbia—called for the Court's interpretation of a different constitutional provision,[1] it was not consolidated with the others, though it was set down for argument immediately after them.

Before any oral argument took place, however, the different parties in all five cases had an opportunity to present their views in writing, for the rules of the Court require the filing of printed briefs in which the legal arguments, historical materials, and pertinent precedents may be brought together. The briefs were filed after each party had designated those portions of the proceedings in the courts below that it wanted printed, so that the Court would have a standard record to which the

---

[1] The due process clause of the Fifth Amendment, rather than the equal protection clause of the Fourteenth Amendment.

lawyers could later refer in both briefs and oral argument.[2]

Because of the massive amount of research they may entail, briefs often can be an important source of information for the Court. Under the adversary system of justice, each side in a case is expected to leave no stone unturned in its search for both factual data and logical arguments supporting its position. Thus, in an indirect way the lawyers engaged in the preparation of briefs function as uncompensated research assistants to the Justices.

In every case, the party that is asking the Supreme Court to reverse a lower court decision must be the first to submit its brief. Then the other side has thirty days to prepare a reply. The briefs are usually quite unlike the papers that were filed originally, when the substance of the controversy was not involved but rather the question of whether the case deserved to be considered at all. Now for the first time the more basic issues are joined. Particularly because some lawyers feel that the Justices often make up their minds irrevocably on the basis of the briefs alone, a sense of now-or-never urgency can often be detected in these documents.

"Amicus Curiae"

On occasion the Supreme Court receives more than two sets of briefs in a case. For there may be someone other than the litigants—perhaps an individual with a similar case pending in a lower court, or an interested organization—who can shed some light on the questions before the Court. The time-honored designation of *amicus curiae* is given to such a person or group.

Under the rules of the Court, the United States Government and all the state governments, as well, have a standing

[2] The actual printing of the Record is done under the supervision of the Clerk's Office of the Supreme Court. Costs are later assessed against the losing party (except for the United States Government, which is generally not liable). Rule 57 of the *Rules of the Supreme Court,* 346 U.S., 1006–07 (1954).

invitation to enter any case as a "friend of the court" without requesting special permission. This arrangement rests on the assumption that there is frequently a strong public interest in the outcome of a case and that private litigants cannot be relied on to argue the case from the standpoint of that interest.

But the situation is different for private individuals or groups not directly involved in a case. For them to be recognized as "friends of the court," it is normally necessary to obtain the approval of both parties in the case. Since the Government of the United States is a party to approximately half of the litigation before the Supreme Court, this means that the Solicitor General, who represents the Department of Justice, occupies a strategic position in determining which *amicus* briefs receive official sanction. His office says that it consents most readily to the filing of an *amicus* brief if "the applicant has a concrete, substantial interest in the decision of the case, and the proposed brief would assist the Court by presenting relevant arguments or materials which would not otherwise be submitted."[3] But in practice the Department of Justice seldom actually withholds its consent. On the rare occasions when it does, the Court may be asked for "leave to file" a brief, and it hardly ever says no.[4]

Until 1949, the Court's policy on *amicus* briefs was even more permissive than it is today. In that year, the Justices amended their rules to tighten the procedure. In part their new stringency reflected exasperation at the number of "friends of the court," forty in all, who had submitted briefs that year in a contempt-of-Congress case.[5] But basically, the stricter policy stemmed from an uneasy feeling that *amicus* briefs had been converted into a device for trying to pressure the Court. This feeling was put into words by a lawyer who served as "reporter" to a Committee of the Supreme Court when it pro-

---

[3] Quoted in Glendon A. Schubert, *Constitutional Politics* (New York: Holt, Rinehart & Winston, 1960), p. 77.

[4] The criteria that apply are described in Rule 42, *Rules of the Supreme Court,* 346 U.S. 993–94 (1954).

[5] *Marshall* v. *United States,* 339 U.S. 933 (1949); *Lawson* v. *United States,* 339 U.S. 934 (1949).

BRIEF FOR AMICI CURIAE

IN THE

Supreme Court of the United States

OCTOBER TERM, 1952

No. 413

SPOTTSWOOD THOMAS BOLLING, ET AL., *Petitioners*

v.

C. MELVIN SHARPE, ET AL.

*ON WRIT OF CERTIORARI TO THE UNITED STATES COURT OF
APPEALS FOR THE DISTRICT OF COLUMBIA CIRCUIT*

AMERICAN COUNCIL ON HUMAN
RIGHTS

AMERICANS FOR DEMOCRATIC ACTION
WASHINGTON CHAPTER

AMERICAN JEWISH COMMITTEE
WASHINGTON CHAPTER

AMERICAN JEWISH CONGRESS COM-
MISSION ON LAW & SOCIAL ACTION
WASHINGTON CHAPTER

CATHOLIC INTERRACIAL COUNCIL
OF WASHINGTON

COMMISSION ON COMMUNITY LIFE OF
THE WASHINGTON FEDERATION OF
CHURCHES

DISTRICT OF COLUMBIA INDUSTRIAL
UNION COUNCIL, C.I.O.

D. C. FEDERATION OF CIVIC
ASSOCIATIONS, INC.

FRIENDS COMMITTEE ON NATIONAL
LEGISLATION

JAPANESE AMERICAN CITIZENS
LEAGUE
WASHINGTON CHAPTER

JEWISH COMMUNITY COUNCIL OF
GREATER WASHINGTON

NATIONAL ASSOCIATION FOR THE
ADVANCEMENT OF COLORED PEOPLE
D. C. BRANCH

UNITARIAN FELLOWSHIP FOR
SOCIAL JUSTICE
WASHINGTON CHAPTER

WASHINGTON BAR ASSOCIATION

WASHINGTON ETHICAL SOCIETY

WASHINGTON FELLOWSHIP

WASHINGTON INTERRACIAL
WORKSHOP

WASHINGTON URBAN LEAGUE

S. WALTER SHINE,
THEODORE C. SORENSEN,
SANFORD H. BOLZ,
SAMUEL B. GRONER,
Counsel.

PRESS OF BYRON S. ADAMS, WASHINGTON, D. C.

Eighteen organizations file a single amicus *brief on the side of the Negroes in the District of Columbia case.*

duced a major overhaul of the rules in 1954. Before 1949, the lawyer said, *amicus* briefs

> had become a vehicle for propaganda efforts. . . . [T]heir emphasis was on the size and importance of the group represented, or on contemporaneous press comment. . . . The brief *amicus curiae* had become essentially an instrumentality designed to exert extrajudicial pressure on judicial decisions. . . .[6]

Yet the new rule, designed to put an end to this situation, was too restrictive for at least one member of the Court. Justice Black thought that both "the public interest and judicial administration would be better served by relaxing rather than tightening the rule against *amicus curiae* briefs." His argument was that "most of the cases before this Court involve matters that affect far more people than the immediate record parties." [7]

Certainly there have been numerous occasions when outside briefs were of great help to the Court. In 1961, for instance, a brief filed by the American Civil Liberties Union as *amicus curiae* paved the way for a major constitutional decision. Although neither of the parties in an obscenity case had thought to raise the point, the civil liberties organization asked the Justices to take a fresh look at an earlier decision which declared that state courts did not have to exclude evidence obtained through unconstitutional search and seizure. The Court adopted the suggestion and announced a landmark decision overturning the old rule.[8]

In the School Segregation Cases, a grand total of twenty-four *amicus* briefs were filed, all except five on the side of the Negroes. Among the organizations that urged the Court to

[6] Frederick Bernays Wiener, "The Supreme Court's New Rules," *Harvard Law Review*, Vol. 68 (November, 1954), p. 80.

[7] 346 U.S. 947. Black's dissenting opinion was registered in 1954, when the Court adopted a new set of rules confirming the *amicus* policy of 1949, except for the rather odd provision that "friend of the court" briefs which did not receive the consent of the parties could now be submitted together with the motion requesting permission to file them.

[8] *Mapp* v. *Ohio*, 367 U.S. 643 (1961), reversing *Wolf* v. *Colorado*, 338 U.S. 25 (1949).

invalidate school segregation were the American Jewish Congress, the American Civil Liberties Union, the American Federation of Teachers, the American Veterans Committee, and the Congress of Industrial Organizations. Their briefs were prepared by men who had long been active in the field of constitutional rights. One of them was Arthur J. Goldberg, who was later appointed to a seat on the Supreme Court.[9] The NAACP worked closely with the *amici* in order to avoid unnecessary duplication.

Solicitor General

Probably the most important *amicus* brief in the school cases was the one filed on behalf of the United States Government. Not only did the Government submit an extensive brief; it also participated, by invitation of the Court, in the oral argument.[10]

All government business in the Supreme Court is in the hands of the Solicitor General of the United States. Although both the Attorney General and the Deputy Attorney General outrank him in the Department of Justice, the Solicitor General possesses a surprising degree of autonomy, for his office has a long tradition that associates it with the Supreme Court almost as much as with the Executive Branch.

The principal responsibility of the Solicitor General is to decide whether to appeal the cases lost by the Government in the lower courts. The decision is in his hands whenever the

[9] Only three years after his appointment as Associate Justice, Goldberg resigned from the Court to become the United States Ambassador to the United Nations. It was one of the few Supreme Court resignations in recent history. Outright resignation involves a complete separation from the Court and its work. Retirement, on the other hand, means that the member, although he is on pension, retains an office in the Supreme Court Building, keeps his former title, and may make himself available for occasional assignment by the Chief Justice to other federal courts.

[10] Ordinarily, *amici* may take part in oral argument only when the parties approve or when the Court grants an appropriate motion. Such motions, says the Court somewhat sourly, "are not favored." Rule 44, *Rules of the Supreme Court*, 346 U.S. 996–97 (1954).

Government must make up its mind on appealing an adverse decision, either to the Court of Appeals or to the Supreme Court.

In the latter instance the Solicitor General is most acutely aware of how different his position is from that of an attorney in private practice. The ordinary lawyer may feel no qualms about going along when a client who has just lost a case blusters, "We'll take it all the way to the Supreme Court!" Even if the Court says no to a petition for Certiorari, nothing will have been lost except money—and the client's money, at that. On the other hand, the lawyer representing the Government has his professional prestige to consider. For through the years the Court has developed trust in the judgment of the Solicitor General. It therefore relies on him not to bring up cases just because some federal agency is chafing at its defeat in a lower court. As a consequence, the Solicitor General can be obstinate to the point of rudeness when importuned to try his luck in the Supreme Court. Because he exercises his discretion in such a responsible manner, a majority of the petitions for Certiorari that he does file are granted—75 percent of them in some years—while the comparable figure for private litigants is only about 10 percent.

If his colleagues in government tend to become greatly exercised when the Solicitor General refuses to prosecute an appeal on their behalf, they are even more upset when he acts to deprive them of a victory already gained. This peculiar situation may arise when the Solicitor General comes to the conclusion that the Government should have lost a case that it actually won in a lower court. In such an instance, he files a "confession of error" with the Supreme Court, asking that the decision below be overruled. The Court nearly always accedes to that request and reverses the decision summarily.[11]

[11] There are, however, exceptions. Many years before he himself became Solicitor General, Archibald L. Cox took a job as an attorney in the Solicitor General's office. In order to buoy the confidence of a new man, it is customary to start him off with a case he cannot possibly lose. Accordingly, Cox's first assignment was a "confession of error" case. He managed, however, to achieve the impossible, and lost. (From interview

Filing of Briefs

Normally, of course, the Solicitor General is just as heavily involved in cases where the United States Government is an *amicus* as when it is actually a party to the litigation. But there were major decisions in the School Segregation Cases that had to be made by various other people, because the office stood vacant for thirteen crucial months, with only an Acting Solicitor General in charge.[12] The situation was further complicated by the fact that, in the course of the school litigation, control of the Presidency shifted not only from one individual to another but from one party to another, for on January 20, 1953, Harry S. Truman was succeeded in the White House by Dwight D. Eisenhower.

It was in the closing days of the Truman administration that the Government's first brief in the School Segregation Cases was filed. There had previously been considerable hesitation in the Department of Justice as to whether the Government should involve itself in the school cases at all. The Solicitor General, Philip B. Perlman, had strongly opposed the idea of submitting a brief, but he did not remain in office long enough to have the last word. After his resignation (for reasons that had nothing to do with the school issue), Robert L. Stern, who succeeded him on an acting basis, convinced Attorney General James P. McGranery that a brief by the Government was indeed in order. McGranery, however, insisted on one

---

with a rueful Solicitor General Cox [now a professor at Harvard Law School], January 6, 1965.)

[12] Robert L. Stern, who was First Assistant to the Solicitor General, served as Acting Solicitor General both before and after the brief tenure of Walter J. Cummings, who was Solicitor General for only three months, from December 2, 1952, to March 1, 1953. Stern's first period as Acting Solicitor General began on August 15, 1952, and extended to the date when Mr. Cummings took office; his second tour of duty began on March 2, 1953, and ended on February 25, 1954, when President Eisenhower commissioned Simon E. Sobeloff (now a judge on the Court of Appeals for the Fourth Circuit) as Solicitor General.

condition: the brief would not be filed until after the presidential election of 1952, to keep school segregation from becoming an issue in the campaign, and also to avoid creating any last-minute problems for the Democratic candidate, Adlai E. Stevenson.

The author of the Government's brief was a Department of Justice attorney, Philip Elman,[13] who was deeply devoted to the cause of civil rights. Elman expressed himself forcefully on the main issue. "Compulsory racial segregation," he said in the brief, was "itself an unconstitutional discrimination," and the "separate but equal" doctrine was in reality a caricature of the Fourteenth Amendment. Yet Elman did not insist that the "separate but equal" doctrine be overruled. Perhaps, he said, the Court would prefer to invalidate school segregation in the various states on the familiar ground that equal facilities were not available to the Negro children. Nor did he press in the brief for the immediate issuance of a decree ordering desegregation forthwith. The Justices, he suggested, might wish to schedule a second round of argument to deal with the specific question of how desegregation could be carried out. One possible method would be to leave it to the Federal District Courts in each locality to develop suitable implementation plans in cooperation with the officials in charge of the school system.

There is reason to believe that the moderate approach Elman adopted was the result of a highly practical assessment of what had to be done in order to avoid losing the case hands down. The apprehension was that not enough support existed in the Court for the kind of uncompromising decision that the NAACP wanted. Only three Justices—Black, Douglas, and Burton—could be counted on to overrule the Plessy decision and order immediate desegregation. Three others, it was thought, were dead set against desegregating elementary and secondary schools. One of these was Chief Justice Vinson, who had gone as far as he would ever go when he voted in favor of desegregating Southern law schools and graduate schools, and the other two were Justices Minton and Reed. The re-

[13] Now a member of the Federal Trade Commission.

maining members of the Court—Frankfurter, Clark, and Jackson—could throw their support to either side. It was to these three, and most particularly to Frankfurter, that Elman directed his brief.

Frankfurter's attitude seems to have been that the Court, might do serious damage to the whole federal judicial system if it tried to supervise school desegregation throughout the South. Desegregation he considered to be an essentially political task that was wholly outside the proper function of the Judicial Branch, especially the Supreme Court. On the other hand, his heart was completely on the side of desegregating the schools. Thus the approach adopted by Elman, who had once served as a law clerk to Frankfurter, was an ingenious effort to give the Justice a way in which he could express his personal condemnation of school segregation while at the same time reserving his position on how desegregation should be put into effect.

Not content with the filing of a brief, the Department of Justice also asked the Court for permission to participate, in the person of Attorney General McGranery, in the oral argument. But the request was turned down, for Chief Justice Vinson felt there was already more than enough pressure on the Court to abandon the "separate but equal" doctrine, which he was resolved to perpetuate. The Government would have been seriously embarrassed if the story of its request and the Court's rebuff had been made public. By mutual agreement, therefore, the Clerk of the Court simply returned to the Department of Justice the letter containing the request, and no public announcement was made. It was as though the Government's petition had never been submitted.

NAACP Briefs

The NAACP, in the briefs that it prepared on behalf of the five sets of Negro litigants, spent little time on enforcement problems. Instead, it chose to emphasize history, marshaling the evidence to prove that the states which ratified the Four-

teenth Amendment understood that it would rule out segregation in public schools. It also attempted to relate the school
cases to the Cold War. "Survival of our country in the present
international situation," said the NAACP, "is inevitably tied
to resolution of this domestic issue."

As it had done in the lower courts, the NAACP called
attention to the findings of social scientists that segregation
inculcates feelings of inequality and inferiority. This argument
was bolstered by an appendix in which thirty-two nationally
prominent social scientists tried to prove that white as well as
Negro children suffer serious psychological damage because
of the superior-inferior relationship in which the two groups
are cast under conditions of segregation. The signers of the
statement included anthropologists, psychiatrists, psycholo-
gists, and sociologists, all with at least some experience in the
field of race relations. Expressing confidence that desegregation could be accomplished without violence, they stated that
the crumbling of the racial barrier might actually usher in a
new era of amicability in relations between Negroes and
whites.

5. Oral Argument

When the Supreme Court agrees to hear a case, it expects more from the parties than the mere submission of printed briefs. Almost invariably, it schedules an hour or two of oral argument as well. That enables the two sides to confront each other's arguments directly. It also allows the Justices to question the opposing attorneys, and by no means infrequently, to debate with them. Oral argument is considered so helpful in the decision-making process that when a Justice is ill and must be absent during the argument in a particular case, he generally refrains from voting on the final outcome even though he may be thoroughly conversant with the issues.

The Justices meet to hear oral argument in an immense courtroom occupying almost 7,500 square feet. Marble pillars, mahogany furnishings, velvet drapes, and thick carpets combine to create an effect of elegance and splendor. Along the sides of the room stand twenty-four magnificent columns with carved marble panels above them, and behind the bench, which is fashioned from mahogany, are four more pillars. The only informal touch comes from the leather chairs on which the Justices sit: no two are alike, for each member of the Court is permitted to select his own. Seats are provided for the public, and special sections are reserved for the press, members of the Supreme Court Bar, and guests of the Justices.

Not always did the Supreme Court hold its sessions in such impressive surroundings. Until 1935, when the present building was completed, the Court's "home" was a much smaller chamber on the first floor of the Capitol, now a Senate hearing room. Prior to that, the Court occupied a far from imposing suite of rooms in the Capitol basement. Justice Harlan Fiske Stone, who was on the Court when the move was made to the new building, was not enthusiastic about the change. The new courtroom, he said, was "almost bombastically pretentious" and "wholly inappropriate for a quiet group of old boys such as the Supreme Court." [1]

From the opening of the Court's term in October until early in spring, the Justices hear oral argument for approximately two weeks each month, reserving the rest of the time for opinion writing and other chores. During the weeks when argument is held, they sit Monday through Thursday for four hours each day—from 10 o'clock in the morning until noon, and then, after a thirty-minute break for lunch, until 2:30 P.M. Friday is set aside for the all-important conference.

This 10:00-to-2:30 schedule is an innovation dating back only to 1961. Before then, the Court had convened each day at high noon, recessing for lunch at 2 o'clock and then reconvening for two more hours, until 4:30. It was still working under this schedule when the argument in the School Segregation Cases began, on December 9, 1952.

Shortly before noon, the lawyers who were to participate in the case entered the courtroom to await the opening of the session. All had prepared carefully for the challenge ahead. The battery of NAACP attorneys had actually organized at Howard University an elaborate mock hearing at which they presented their arguments to law professors and subjected themselves to the kind of merciless questioning that could be

[1] The Foundation of the Federal Bar Association, *Equal Justice Under Law: The Supreme Court in American Life* (Washington, 1965), p. 114.

expected from the Justices. Some of the other lawyers, too, had staged dress rehearsals for the drama that was soon to begin, reciting their arguments to whatever audience was available.[2]

At about the same time that the lawyers were settling themselves in their places, Chief Justice Vinson and the other members of the Court were assembling in a tiny anteroom nearby to be helped into their judicial robes. As they always do before a conference or a public session, they shook hands with one another. When they were ready to enter the courtroom, a guard pressed a buzzer. The Court Crier, seated at a desk immediately beneath the bench, jumped to his feet, rapped his gavel, and called out, "All rise!"

In groups of three, the Justices came through the parted curtains adjacent to the bench and stood behind their chairs. The Crier proclaimed: "The Honorable, the Chief Justice and the Associate Justices of the Supreme Court of the United States." Then, chanting rather than speaking, he intoned the traditional cry, beginning with the old French word for "hear ye":

> Oyez! Oyez! Oyez! All persons having business before the Honorable, the Supreme Court of the United States, are invited to draw near and give their attention, for the Court is now sitting. God save the United States and this Honorable Court.[3]

When the Crier rapped his gavel again, everyone was seated. The courtroom was filled to capacity, as it almost

[2] An authority on appellate practice has given this description of the methods most commonly used for such dress rehearsals: "Some lawyers prefer to try out their preliminary efforts on The Little Woman. Others inflict it on a moot court of generous friends. Still others undertake the task in decent seclusion, preferably at night. . . . And a fourth method is to use a sound tape . . . and then play back one's golden words." Frederick Bernays Wiener, *Briefing and Arguing Federal Appeals* (Washington: Bureau of National Affairs, 1961), p. 308.

[3] It is probably an apocryphal story, but it has been said that during the early days of the New Deal era, when the Court was busily invalidating some of the most important legislation enacted by Congress at the urging of President Franklin D. Roosevelt, a Democratic Court Crier, his subconscious in complete command, ended his chant with "God save the United States *from* this Honorable Court."

always is when momentous cases are argued or when important decisions are expected. Of the some three hundred-odd spectators, nearly half were Negroes. In the wide marble corridors outside the courtroom, approximately five hundred more people waited in line. Half of them, too, were Negroes.

Before the school cases could be taken up, argument had to be completed in another case for which time had run out on the previous day. That was soon over and done with, and the moment for which everyone had been waiting finally arrived. The Chief Justice looked down at the paper before him and read: "Case No. 8, *Oliver Brown and others* v. *the Board of Education of Topeka, Shawnee County, Kansas.*" The Clerk said: "Counsel are present." Vinson then recognized the attorney who was to begin the argument. "Mr. Carter," he said.

Robert Carter, the NAACP lawyer who had handled the Topeka case from the start, began with the conventional statement orienting the Justices on the route by which the litigation had reached the Supreme Court:

> This case is here on direct appeal pursuant to Title 22, Section 1253, 2201 (b), from the final judgment of a statutory three-judge court . . . for the District of Kansas, denying appellants' . . . application for a permanent injunction to restrain the enforcement of Chapter 72, 1724, of the General Statutes of Kansas on the grounds of that statute's fatal conflict with the requirements of the guarantees of the Fourteenth Amendment.[4]

Carter then launched into a description of the findings by the court below. Although he consulted notes once in a while, for the most part he spoke extemporaneously, because the Rules of the Court warn counsel that the Justices look "with disfavor on any oral argument that is read from a prepared text."[5]

---

[4] On one occasion, an inexperienced lawyer plunged immediately into the substance of his argument, forgetting the preliminary statement about the route that his case had traveled. The Chief Justice interrupted to inquire, "But how did you get here?" Came the reply: "By bus, your Honor."

[5] Rule 44, *Rules of the Supreme Court*, 346 U.S. 995 (1954).

Questions from the Bench

Carter had not advanced very far into his argument when he was interrupted by one of the Justices. Questions from the Bench often make oral argument a shattering ordeal for the lawyers. The effect on those who are inadequately prepared is devastating, for the members of the Court are adept at peeling away the rhetorical coating that may have been used to conceal weaknesses and inconsistencies in the briefs. Yet even the lawyer who has done his homework conscientiously can never know when a carefully planned and even memorized argument may be derailed by a Justice who interrupts to announce: "That's all very interesting, but what *I* want to know is . . ." [6]

The first Justice to interrupt Carter was Sherman Minton. His question gave the lawyer no difficulty. All Minton wanted was clarification of the decision in the three-judge District Court.

> MINTON: Mr. Carter, I do not know whether I have followed you on all the facts on this. Was there a finding that the only basis of classification was race or color?
>
> CARTER: It was admitted—the appellees admitted in their answer—that the only reason that they would not permit Negro children to attend the 18 white schools was because they were Negroes.
>
> MINTON: Then we accept on this record that the only showing is that the classification here was solely on race and color?
>
> CARTER: Yes, sir. I think the State itself concedes this is so. . . .

[6] The volume of questions from the bench can be inferred from some friendly advice that lawyers are given in an unofficial manual on Supreme Court practice: "Experience suggests that when one hour is allowed [for argument], counsel would do well not to plan an argument taking over 35 to 40 minutes; when 30 minutes are allowed, not over 20 minutes." Robert L. Stern and Eugene Gressman, *Supreme Court Practice* (Washington: Bureau of National Affairs, 1962), p. 359.

The argument had begun at 1:35 P.M., only twenty-five
minutes before the luncheon break. Carter therefore had not
made much progress in his argument before the Chief Justice
rose from his seat and said that the Court would take its recess.

At 2:30, when the Justices returned from lunch, Carter
resumed his argument and almost at once ran into a barrage
of questions from Felix Frankfurter, the member of the Court
whom lawyers feared most. The "little Justice"—he was only
5 feet 5 inches tall—was a great admirer of all things British,
including the practice in the High Court of England of rely-
ing so heavily on oral argument that written briefs are not
even asked for. Frankfurter's practice was to ignore the briefs
entirely until after he had listened to the oral argument.

During the lawyers' presentations in the School Segregation Cases, Frankfurter was in his element. He interrupted
constantly with barbed remarks, expressions of pained incre-
dulity, and questions phrased in the inimitable Frankfurter
literary style, a blend of sesquipedalian vocabulary with possibly the most involuted syntax of the twentieth century. And
to make matters worse for the hapless attorneys, a particularly
damaging question was often accompanied by a contemptuous
gesture: Frankfurter would throw himself back in his combination rocker-swivel chair, a look of utter disgust on his face,
and pay absolutely no attention to the answer that his question had elicited, preferring instead to chat with one of his
colleagues.[7]

Right after the lunchtime break, Frankfurter was hector-
ing the NAACP lawyer. "Are you saying that we can say that

[7] The Justices frequently talk among themselves while the Court
is in session. The story is told about the lawyers in one case who thought
it might help them to know what the Justices were saying to each other.
They proceeded to retain a lip-reader to report the content of the
whispers exchanged in the course of the argument in their case. During
a lengthy series of questions put by Justice Frankfurter to one of the
attorneys, Justice Douglas leaned over to one of his colleagues and
whispered something to him. The lawyers turned eagerly to the lip-
reader to learn what Douglas had said. "He said," the man replied, "that
he wished Frankfurter would stop talking for a few minutes and give the
lawyer a chance."

'separate but equal' is not a doctrine that is relevant at the primary school level? Is that what you are saying?" he demanded. Justice Douglas tried to help the lawyer out. "I think you are saying," he ventured, "that segregation may be all right in street cars and railroad cars and restaurants, but . . . education is different from that." The lawyer found the Douglas paraphrase to his liking. "Yes, sir," he replied. Douglas continued: "That is your argument, is it not? Isn't that your argument in this case?" Again a grateful "yes" from Carter.

Frankfurter, however, was not even moderately impressed. "But how *can* that be your argument . . . ?" he cried, and the lawyer was once again on his own.[8]

A Sharp Break?

Whatever could be said of Frankfurter's manner, the difficulty he was pointing out was a real one. As he analyzed the situation, the course of action that Carter was urging on the Court—a holding that segregation in public schools violated the Fourteenth Amendment—would mean a sharp break with even the recent past, for all the cases in which the Court had ordered an end to segregation had rested simply on the finding that equal facilities had not been provided, not that segregated facilities could. *never* be equal. Obviously Frankfurter was extremely reluctant to have the Court indicate that countless decisions of past years had rested on an erroneous interpretation of the Fourteenth Amendment.

At least one of his colleagues seemed to think that Frankfurter was creating a problem where none actually existed. Justice Burton said he saw no reason why the repudiation of

[8] Doubtless Carter would have appreciated an anecdote once related by Justice Jackson. As the story goes, the judge in a British appellate tribunal said to a lawyer in the course of a learned argument: "I have been listening to you now for four hours and I am bound to say I am none the wiser." The barrister shot back: "Oh, I know that, my Lord, but I had hoped you would be better informed." "Advocacy Before the United States Supreme Court," *Cornell Law Quarterly*, Vol. 37 (Fall, 1951), p. 11.

the separate but equal doctrine in education would necessarily imply that any previous decisions had been wrong. He
explained that conditions had changed so much since the
Plessy decision—in education, for example, public schools had
been a distinct rarity in 1896—that what had previously been
a valid interpretation might no longer be one.

As the argument proceeded, it seemed at times as though
the case being made by Carter was important mainly as a
springboard for individual Justices to develop their own tentative hypotheses and allow these to be examined in a free-for-
all debate. There was nothing unusual in this. Members of the
Court are never hesitant about expressing themselves freely
as a case is being argued, for there are neither witnesses nor
jurors present who might be influenced by a frank expression
of judicial attitudes.

Moreover, the questions asked by Justices during oral
argument, or even the comments they make, are by no means
reliable indices of how they will actually vote in a case. Often
the questions are merely designed to draw out the attorneys.
Or they may be nothing more than reflections of a preliminary
attitude that will be altered before the case is finally decided.

As Carter was entitled to do, he reserved a portion of his
time for rebuttal. The hour had come for the Court to hear
the arguments on the other side.

Speaking in defense of the Kansas statute was the State's
Assistant Attorney General, Paul E. Wilson. The lawyer insisted that it would be impossible to declare segregated
schools unconstitutional without striking down the Plessy doctrine at the same time. His strategy was obvious. Playing on
the traditional reluctance of the Court to overturn long-standing constitutional doctrine, he was trying to make it as difficult
as possible for the Justices to decide against him. Thus he
emphasized the fact that in the Plessy opinion separate schools
were mentioned specifically as an example of the kind of segregation that was lawful. And for much the same reason he
insisted that by breaking with the Plessy precedent the Court
would be administering a slap to no fewer than twenty-one

states—seventeen that *required* segregation in the public schools and four that specifically *sanctioned* it.

After Wilson had completed his argument, Carter returned to the lectern, this time under the Court rule permitting rebuttal. Again he tried to persuade the Justices that a decision in favor of the Negro litigants would really be a logical development of the principles laid down in recent cases, rather than something new and revolutionary, as Wilson had insisted.

It was 3:15 P.M. when Carter concluded his rebuttal. The argument in the Topeka case had consumed only a little more than an hour of the ten hours that the Court had set aside for the School Segregation Cases.

Marshall v. Davis

Without any pause, the Court turned its attention to the second school case on its docket, the one involving Clarendon County, South Carolina. The lawyers in this suit were better known than those whom they replaced at the counsel table. On the anti-segregation side was Thurgood Marshall, the director-counsel of the NAACP and the best-known Negro lawyer in the country. And Marshall had an opponent who was worthy of his mettle: John W. Davis. who in the course of his illustrious career had been Solicitor General, Ambassador to England, and the presidential candidate of the Democratic Party (against Calvin Coolidge in 1924). No man had argued as many cases before the Supreme Court as he had, and only six months earlier Davis had won a spectacular legal victory when the Justices endorsed his argument that President Truman had acted without constitutional authorization in seizing the steel mills to end a major national strike.[9]

Marshall amplified and supplemented the points that had

[9] *Youngstown Sheet & Tube Co.* v. *Sawyer*, 343 U.S. 579 (1952). The case is described in Alan F. Westin, *The Anatomy of a Constitutional Law Case* (New York: Macmillan, 1958).

already been made in the Topeka case. Segregation, he said, was unconstitutional, in and of itself. From the pupils' point of view, in fact, it was even more detrimental than discrepancies in the physical plant of a school or in teaching standards. Futhermore, the Court not only had the power to outlaw it but even the duty to do so, since the manifest purpose of the Fourteenth Amendment was to eradicate all racial distinctions.

As Marshall viewed it, the Plessy doctrine had to be repudiated because it rested on the classification of pupils by race. Many cases had established the principle that classification of any kind could be reconciled with the Fourteenth Amendment only if it rested on a rational basis and served a legitimate legislative purpose. In Marshall's view, South Carolina had failed dismally to establish either of these facts, although both had to be proved for school segregation to continue.

When it was his turn to speak, Davis hit hard at the points made by Marshall. Did segregation actually inflict psychological damage? Little had been proven by devices like the "doll test," for the results of the test were substantially the same whether Negro children had gone to segregated schools or to integrated schools. Was the Fourteenth Amendment really intended by Congress to ban school segregation? If so, Congress would never have allowed segregated schools to be maintained in the District of Columbia. And to Davis's way of thinking, the classification of school children by race was no less reasonable than their classification by sex, age, or mental capacity.

Davis contended that it made no difference if conditions had changed in the country either since the adoption of the Fourteenth Amendment or since the rendering of the Plessy decision. "Changed conditions," he said, "cannot broaden the terminology of the Constitution . . . . " The lawyer stressed that the Federal Judiciary was totally unsuited to deal with problems like public education; such matters should be handled at the state and county level. Clarendon County was in the process of equalizing the facilities of its Negro and white schools, he asserted, and the principle of local self-government should not be undermined by Supreme Court action that would impede this process.

The Human Factor

The South Carolina case, pitting two celebrated advocates against each other, was the high point of the two days of argument. But moments of high drama were yet to come: the lawyer for the Negroes in Virginia,[10] pleading with the Justices not to base any integration order on a finding that educational facilities were unequal, for that way the Negro children might one day have to be segregated again upon a showing that facilities had been equalized; the attorney for the Negroes in Washington,[11] cautioning the Court that fundamental freedoms in the nation's capital should not be left to the tender mercies of Congress, for "never in the history of this country have the individual liberties of a citizen been entrusted to the legislatures"; and, on the other side, Virginia's Attorney General[12] warning that the very existence of the school system in his state would be imperiled by a desegregation order, for there was sure to be firm resistance against the levying of taxes or the issuance of bonds to finance schools to be attended by both Negroes and whites; and the Assistant Corporation Counsel of the District of Columbia,[13] asserting disarmingly that the Justices could see with their own eyes what a fine school system had been created for Negroes in Washington: they had only to look at George E. C. Hayes, a Negro lawyer on the other side, a product of that very system.

And there was drama in the questioning by the Justices,

[10] Spottswood W. Robinson, III, who later became a federal district judge in the District of Columbia.

[11] James M. Nabrit, Jr., who later was named president of Howard University and still later the permanent United States Delegate to the United Nations Security Council.

[12] J. Lindsay Almond, Jr., now a Judge on the United States Court of Customs and Patent Appeals. See p. 96, n. 21.

[13] Milton D. Korman.

too. During the argument in the Delaware case, for example, one of the State's lawyers noted that the Negro children were already enrolled in the previously all-white school, in obedience to an order by a state court. In a soft Alabama accent that had been completely unaffected by twenty-five years in Washington, Justice Black noted drily, "I thought the argument was that they could not get in, that it would disrupt the schools."

At 3:50 P.M. on Thursday, December 11, 1952, it was all over. The argument, stretching over three days, had consumed all but half an hour of the ten hours that had been allotted.[14] Although the lawyers had understood fully the size of the stakes involved, they had permitted themselves no passionate outbursts and only a minimum of forensic flourishes. In the tradition of appellate advocacy, they had studiously avoided the kind of flamboyant rhetoric that is expected in jury trials. Experienced in Supreme Court practice, they knew that the Justices tended to look down on displays of histrionics. There were, however, a few occasions when they became so engrossed in their argument that they had to be reminded that time was running out. This is done in the Supreme Court through a system of warning lights on the lectern. When a lawyer has only five minutes of his time left, the Marshal or his assistant presses a button to turn on a white light. When a red light is switched on, that means the time has expired and the lawyer must stop—and without a moment's delay. It has been said that Chief Justice Hughes once called time on a lawyer in the middle of the word "if." [15]

After the conclusion of the argument in any case, the

[14] Two hours were allowed by the Court for each of the five cases since all had been placed on the Regular Calendar, which is reserved for litigation of any complexity. Cases that are "of such a character as not to justify extended argument" appear on the Summary Calendar, which permits only one hour for each case. No more than one lawyer can argue for each side in cases on the Summary Calendar. Rule 44, *Rules of the Supreme Court*, 346 U.S. 996 (1954).

[15] Edwin McElwain, "The Business of the Supreme Court as Conducted by Chief Justice Hughes," *Harvard Law Review*, Vol. 63 (November, 1949), p. 17.

Justices proceed immediately to the next case on their schedule. They give no indication in the meanwhile of what their
decision will be or even when it will be rendered. Thus, when
the argument on school segregation had been completed, the
Justices turned their attention at once to another quite un-
related case. But the words of the Fourteenth Amendment
argument were still ringing, and the impressions that had been
formed would doubtless be carried into the conference room,
the place where Supreme Court decisions are made.

Making Haste Slowly

On Saturday, December 13, 1952, the Justices met in conference to start discussing the School Segregation Cases
argued earlier that week. In all likelihood, this was the first
of many conferences devoted to the school cases, for although
the argument took place early in December and although the
first conference was held only a few days later, no decision
would be announced, as it turned out, until the following June.

Of course, the votes taken and the precise points that
were made in the various conferences are not matters of
public record and cannot be known with any degree of certainty unless the papers of individual Justices who took part
are ever published.[16] What *is* known is that the members of
the Court came to the conclusion that it was impossible to
arrive at any decision before the end of the 1952–1953 term.
They needed more negotiation and more discussion—and also
more facts.

On the next-to-last Opinion Day of the term the Justices
made known their decision not to decide. In the courtroom sat

[16] Information on scores of conferences extending over seventeen
years was made available to Merlo J. Pusey for his biography of Charles
Evans Hughes. So many cats were let out of the bag in the two-volume
work (*Charles Evans Hughes,* New York: Columbia University Press,
1963) that some of the Justices who are presently on the Court have
given serious thought to the possibility of ordering their papers destroyed
upon their deaths.

a number of NAACP lawyers as well as others involved in the school cases. They had for good reason chosen to be present that day. Since the Court invariably disposes of all argued cases before recessing for the summer, there was an excellent chance that the decision on segregation would be announced. The reading of opinions began, and seven decisions were handed down, on issues ranging from the procedure for classifying conscientious objectors to the practice of illegal price discrimination. There was even a civil rights case, though it had nothing to do with schools.[17]

After Justice Douglas had read the opinion in that civil rights case, Chief Justice Vinson dashed the hopes of those who were waiting for the verdict on school segregation by bringing the Opinion Day to an end with the routine closing announcement: "The other orders of the Court have been certified by the Chief Justice and filed with the Clerk and will not be announced orally."

But as the lawyers and other spectators were streaming out of the courtroom, attendants were posting, in various strategic locations in the Court building, those "other orders of the Court" that the Chief Justice had referred to before adjourning the session. The mimeographed Order Lists usually contain little more than notations of Certiorari Petitions and Jurisdictional Statements on which the Justices have acted. This time, however, the lawyers who stopped by one of the bulletin boards to glance at the Orders, as well as the news-

[17] *District of Columbia* v. *Thompson Co.*, 346 U.S. 100 (1953). The case involved the legality of a criminal prosecution against a District of Columbia restaurant for refusing to provide service to Negroes. The Justices reversed a lower court holding that the laws penalizing such conduct had been superseded by subsequent legislation. Their decision was unanimous, but it was arrived at by an 8-0 vote instead of a 9-0 vote, since Justice Jackson did not participate in the case. Although such non-participation is sometimes due to illness, a Justice may also decide to "recuse" himself and remain out of a case for other reasons: perhaps he had once provided legal counsel for one of the parties in the case, or his family may have a financial interest in the outcome. Whatever the circumstance, there is no procedure for *compelling* non-participation; the question of recusancy is one for the Justice himself to decide.

men in the press room, saw at a glance that the Order List today was far from routine, for it included an announcement that the School Segregation Cases had been disposed of, though in a fashion that no one had predicted.

Instead of deciding the cases one way or the other, the Court revealed that it was still in need of more information, despite the ten hours of argument already held and the hundreds of pages of briefs and records already filed. The cases would have to be argued again in the fall with respect to particular questions on which further elucidation was desired.

Historical Research

To answer some of the questions on which the Court wanted additional briefs and oral argument, the lawyers on both sides would have to do extensive historical research. The very first subject on which the Court sought guidance was whether the Congress that had submitted the Fourteenth Amendment to the states, and the state legislatures and conventions that had ratified the Amendment, had understood that the effect of their action would be to invalidate school segregation.

And the history assignment given to the lawyers did not end there. It seemed that the Justices were not sure that everything would be settled even if proof could be provided that the constitutional intent had not been to abolish educational segregation. They still wanted to know whether the Fourteenth Amendment empowered Congress to abolish such segregation,[18] or whether the Amendment empowered the courts, "in light of future conditions, to construe [it] as abolishing such segregation of its own force." And even if the intent had not been to authorize either Congress or the courts to put an end to school segregation, might the Amendment

[18] Section 5 of the Fourteenth Amendment had provided that "Congress shall have power to enforce, by appropriate legislation, the provisions of this article."

nonetheless be judicially construed to abolish segregation in
public schools?

The assistance of counsel was solicited also on some practical matters. "Assuming it is decided that segregation in
public schools violates the Fourteenth Amendment," the
Justices invited suggestions about the kind of a decree that
should be formulated.[19] What, in other words, should they do
after making a finding of fact that school segregation violated
the Fourteenth Amendment? Were they compelled to order
immediate desegregation, or did they have discretion to move
more slowly and "permit an effective gradual adjustment to
be brought about from existing segregated systems to arrangements not based on color distinctions?"

As if the Court had not imposed a sufficient burden on
the attorneys, it also requested even more specific advice on
implementation. In the event a gradual adjustment would be
permitted, it asked, precisely how should this be accomplished? Should the Court "formulate detailed decrees [and]
if so what specific issues should the decrees reach"? Or should
it perhaps follow a different course of action and appoint a
"special master" to take evidence and then recommend what
should go into the decrees?[20] Another alternative that the
Court wanted the lawyers to consider—especially interesting
in view of the ultimate implementation decree that was issued
in 1955—was summed up this way:

> Should this Court remand to the courts of first instance
> with directions to frame decrees in this case and if so what

[19] A "decree" is similar in equity cases (such as the School Segregation Cases) to a "judgment" in other cases. In each instance, the Court
announces the legal consequences of the facts it has found to be true.

[20] In equity cases, the Supreme Court—and other courts as well—
occasionally appoints "special masters," sometimes known as "masters in
chancery," to assist it by drawing up a proposed decree. In order to
facilitate his search for the facts needed to determine the nature of that
decree, the master is permitted to conduct hearings at which testimony
is taken under oath. A recent case in which the Supreme Court employed
the services of a special master was *Arizona* v. *California*, posing the
question of how much water each of the two parties could use from the
Colorado River. 373 U.S. 546 (1963).

general directions should the decrees of this Court include and what procedures should the courts of first instance follow in arriving at the specific terms of more detailed decrees?

Not only were the lawyers for the parties in the case asked to suggest answers to these questions, but the Attorney General of the United States was also specifically invited "to take part in the oral argument and to file an additional brief if he so desired." [21] Unlike the situation that had obtained a year earlier, Chief Justice Vinson had been unable to convince his colleagues that the Government should not be encouraged to take too prominent a part in the school cases. The Court scheduled reargument for Monday, October 12, 1953. Four months of preparation time would thus be available to the lawyers who represented the states, the private litigants, and the United States of America.

[21] The text of the "memorandum decision" in which the Supreme Court assigned the School Segregation Cases for reargument and asked for answers to specific questions can be found in 345 U.S. 972 (1953).

6. Round Two

The decision to postpone conclusive action on the School Segregation Cases was intensely frustrating both to the litigants and to the lawyers, who had labored so hard the first time around. Now there would have to be new briefs, new oral arguments, and once again the suspense of waiting for the Justices to announce a decision.

But among the NAACP lawyers the initial feeling of disappointment soon gave way to a more positive reaction. For the lawyers came to the conclusion that the questions put by the Court really pointed to the possibility of a victory of sizeable proportions. Their reasoning was that the Court had indicated by its questions a readiness to ignore the mass of judicial precedent sanctioning the separate but equal principle. Since the ultimate decision would thus almost surely rest on the original intent of those who had framed the Fourteenth Amendment, the subject of debate would now be the constitutional text and not the judicial gloss that had been placed upon it in earlier Supreme Court cases.

In the view of Thurgood Marshall and his colleagues, a glittering opportunity was available: to win perhaps the most important constitutional case of the century by proving that the framers of the Fourteenth Amendment intended to prohibit public school segregation. Lurking in the background, of course, was the possibility that it might go the other way, if the historical research indicated that racially segregated schools were meant to be unaffected by the guarantees of the Fourteenth Amendment. A historian who did extensive work for the NAACP quoted Marshall as saying that what looked like a "golden gate" might "turn out to be a booby trap with a bomb in it." [1]

To arrange for the massive study that would now have to be undertaken, Marshall turned to some of the most accomplished experts in constitutional history and constitutional law. The names of the men whose services he enlisted read like a *Who's Who* of constitutional scholars.[2] Funds to finance their research came not only from the NAACP itself but also from labor unions and private donors as well.

With neither money nor talent in short supply, the historical record underwent a meticulous combing. But, as so often happens in such research, much of the evidence uncovered lent itself to different interpretations. One example concerned the Civil Rights Act of 1866, which Congress had enacted only a few months before approving the Fourteenth Amendment. The House had specifically eliminated from the Act a prohibition against state segregation laws, and it had done so at the behest of John A. Bingham, the Ohio Congressman who later helped write the Fourteenth Amendment. How should this historical evidence be interpreted? Had the same Congressman who opposed the prohibition of segregation by statute understood the Fourteenth Amendment to be more comprehensive? Or had he intended that the bounds of the constitutional provision should be much the same as those of the statute? [3]

[1] Alfred H. Kelly, "The School Desegregation Cases," in John A. Garraty, ed., *Quarrels That Have Shaped the Constitution* (New York: Harper and Row, 1964), p. 260.

[2] Included were Horace Bond, Robert K. Carr, Robert Cushman, Jr., John P. Frank, John Hope Franklin, Walter Gellhorn, Howard Jay Graham, Alfred H. Kelly, Milton R. Konvitz, and C. Vann Woodward. *Ibid.*, pp. 260–61.

[3] *Ibid.*, p. 262.

Law-office History

As they delved into the ambiguous historical records, the researchers for the NAACP were by no means acting in the manner of detached and disinterested pursuers after truth. Far from this, they were frankly hunting for evidence that would substantiate a preconceived conclusion: that segregated public schools were irreconcilable with the Fourteenth Amendment. One of the scholars who participated in the work has written with candor about the process that took place:

> It is not that we were engaged in formulating lies; there was nothing as crude and naïve as that. But we were using facts, emphasizing facts, bearing down on facts, sliding off facts, quietly ignoring facts, and above all interpreting facts in a way to do what Marshall said we had to do—"get by those boys down there." [4]
>
> [The brief that emerged] was, of course, not history in any professional sense; rather it was legal advocacy. . . . It sought to place the most favorable gloss upon the critical historical evidence that the Association's staff and advisers could develop without going beyond the facts. [5]
>
> [What we produced] was a piece of highly selective and carefully prepared law-office history. It presented, indeed, a great deal of perfectly valid constitutional history. But it also manipulated history in the best tradition of American advocacy, carefully marshaling every possible scrap of evidence in favor of the desired interpretation and just as carefully doctoring all the evidence to the contrary, either by suppressing it when that seemed plausible, or by distorting it when suppression was not possible. [6]

Doubtless it was also true that the briefs on the other side were just as slanted, and that their authors, too,

[4] Alfred H. Kelly, "An Inside View of *Brown* v. *Board*," Address to Annual Meeting of American Historical Association, Washington, D. C., December 28, 1961 (mimeographed).

[5] Kelly, "The School Desegregation Cases," *op. cit.*, p. 264.

[6] Kelly, "Clio and the Court: An Illicit Love Affair," in Philip B. Kurland, ed., *The Supreme Court Review, 1965* (Chicago: University of Chicago Press, 1965), p. 144.

"doctored, distorted, twisted, and suppressed historical evidence in as competent a fashion as did the NAACP." [7] But for neither the NAACP nor the Southerners did any of this create too painful a conflict in values. Both sets of researchers accepted the theory that the essence of the adversary system is the presentation of the strongest possible case for each of the contending parties, on the premise that it is for the judge, not the lawyer, to decide where the truth is. Accordingly, the Supreme Court was presented with briefs that examined identical historical material and emerged with two sets of conclusions that could not have been more at variance with each other. [8]

A House Divided

None of the actual parties to the litigation had as much trouble preparing briefs as did the United States Government, which was participating as *amicus curiae*. The Government found it necessary, in fact, to ask for a postponement of the deadline for filing its brief, though any delay would mean that the oral argument would have to be put off to a later date. Acting on behalf of the Government, Attorney General Herbert R. Brownell obtained the consent of all the other attorneys in the cases and then petitioned for the postponement. The petition was granted by the Court. December 7 was selected as the new date for the reargument.

A major policy conflict was responsible for holding up

[7] *Ibid.*

[8] Only in one respect—voluminousness—were the briefs similar. The NAACP took 235 printed pages to cover its interpretation of the historical materials, and (to choose just one example on the other side) the South Carolina brief filled 90 pages, not counting a 145-page appendix. The Department of Justice was even more verbose, with its brief occupying 188 pages plus a historical appendix more than twice that long. The documents submitted on the adoption of the Fourteenth Amendment have been called "the most extensive presentation of historical materials ever made to the Court." Alexander M. Bickel, "The Original Understanding and the Segregation Decision," *Harvard Law Review*, Vol. 69 (November, 1955), p. 6.

the submission of the Government's brief. Assistant Attorney General J. Lee Rankin and others in the Department of Justice favored the adoption of a strong stand against school segregation. From the standpoint of desirable public policy, they saw only one position that the United States Government could possibly adopt: vigorous condemnation of the color line in any activity of government, including public school segregation. And they had no doubt whatever that such segregation was impermissible under a correct interpretation of the Constitution.

But within the same Administration there were spokesmen for a very different point of view. Ever since 1948, when ardent segregationists staged a walkout at the Democratic National Convention to protest the adoption of a strong civil rights plank, some Republicans had been intrigued by the possibility that at least a few Southern states might one day be attracted into the GOP column. The party strategists who thought along these lines saw the school cases as a potential source of danger for the Republicans, since an outspoken anti-segregation brief might dash for many years to come any realistic hope of breaking up the Solid South.

By no means did all of the Republican leaders favor a strategy oriented to the South. Some felt that it would be far wiser to compete for the powerful Negro vote in the urban states of the North and prepare the ground at the same time for a major organizational effort among Negroes in the South when racial disfranchisement began to crumble. A strong anti-segregation brief by a Republican Justice Department seemed an ideal way to begin.

Numerous conferences were held by Administration officials to hammer out the policy that the Government would adopt in its brief. A compromise finally resulted. On the one hand, the brief said that the legislative history did "not conclusively establish that the Congress which proposed the Fourteenth Amendment specifically understood . . . it would abolish racial segregation in the public schools . . . . " On the other hand, it insisted that the Amendment had been intended to establish "the broad constitutional principle of full and complete equality of all persons under the law," and that no significance could be attached to the absence of more explicit wording:

> Concerned as they were with securing to the Negro freedmen these fundamental rights of liberty and equality, the members of Congress did not pause to enumerate in detail all the specific applications of the basic principle which the Amendment incorporated into the Constitution.

And what about the intent of the state legislatures? Here, too, said the Department of Justice, the evidence was inconclusive, for the available materials were "too sparse, and the specific references to education too few . . . ."

Nowhere in the entire 188-page Government brief was there a flat statement urging the Court to invalidate public school segregation as a violation of the Constitution. Attorney General Herbert R. Brownell had seen to that. Neither was there any conclusion as to the intention of the framers. Moreover, instead of recommending speed in the conversion to desegregated schools should the Court decide the cases in favor of the Negro litigants, the Government had this to say: "If the Court holds that laws providing for separate schools are unconstitutional, it should remand the instant cases to the lower courts with directions to carry out the Court's decision as the particular circumstances permit."

But the document still managed in some places to breathe a spirit of egalitarian commitment. "The primary and pervasive purpose of the Fourteenth Amendment," it said, "was to secure for Negroes full and complete equality before the law and to abolish all legal distinctions based on race or color." Moreover, the Court should not be content to determine simply "whether there is equality as between *schools;* the Constitution requires that there be equality as between *persons.*" [9]

Attorney General Brownell might have gone further in

[9] Emphasis added.

this direction, but he said that he saw no point in including arguments which were sure to be eliminated by the White House. As a newsman who was close to the Department of Justice put it: "The truth is probably that . . . Brownell would personally have liked to include a direct statement on the unconstitutionality of segregation but did not believe President Eisenhower would approve it." [10]

When the Government's brief was completed, copies were dispatched to the Clerk's Office of the Supreme Court for distribution to the individual Justices. With the other briefs already in, everything was now in order for the reargument that the Court had requested at the end of the previous term.

Earl Warren to the Court

Neither the Government brief nor any of the others was destined to be read by the Chief Justice whose Court had requested that the new briefs be prepared. Just one month before the date set for reargument, Fred M. Vinson died. Thus the Justices who opposed judicial invalidation of school segregation were suddenly left without a leader. President Eisenhower now had to designate a new Chief Justice, either choosing one of the eight Associate Justices or, as is done much more frequently, reaching outside the Court for his appointee.[11]

[10] Anthony Lewis, *Portrait of a Decade: The Second American Revolution* (New York: Random House, 1964), p. 27. The same reporter, who later became the Supreme Court correspondent of *The New York Times*, adds: "The Attorney General did advise the President that [Assistant Attorney General] Rankin, if asked by a member of the Supreme Court during the oral argument what the Justice Department's position was, would say that segregation should be struck down. The President evidently made no objection, and the question was asked and answered as planned." *Ibid.*, pp. 27–28. (For the question and answer referred to, see *infra*, p. 96.

[11] Most Presidents seem reluctant to pick a man already on the Court for fear that there will be bruised feelings on the part of the other seven. Only three of the fourteen Chief Justices have been promoted from the ranks: Edward D. White, Harlan Fiske Stone, and Charles Evans Hughes. Hughes, of course, had left the Court in 1916 to run for the presidency, and before his appointment as Chief Justice had served in a number of important positions including that of Secretary of State.

Instead of promoting an Associate Justice, Mr. Eisenhower did indeed look elsewhere for a new Chief Justice. He decided on a man who was one of the most attractive figures in American politics: Earl Warren, Governor of California. Warren was so popular in his state that on three occasions he had managed to win the gubernatorial nomination of the Democratic party as well as that of his own Republican party. So impressed had the Republicans been with his vote-getting ability that they had given him the vice-presidential nomination in 1948.

Warren was popular with Mr. Eisenhower, too. The President remembered with gratitude that at the Republican National Convention in 1952 the Governor had led the deeply divided California delegation into his camp, thus assuring him the presidential nomination. Mr. Eisenhower seemed delighted at the opportunity to repay a political debt. Of Warren's political and social philosophy he knew little and seemed to care less.[12]

Since Congress was not in session at the time of Vinson's death, the President was unable to send Warren's name to the Senate for the necessary confirmation. The Constitution provides, however, that under such circumstances the President may make a recess appointment, authorizing the nominee to serve through the end of the next session of Congress. If by then the Senate has not voted to confirm the nomination, a second recess appointment may be made, but no compensation can be paid to the appointee for this period of service.

President Eisenhower incurred some criticism for deciding to make a recess appointment to the Court instead of allowing the Chief Justice's seat to remain vacant until Congress reconvened. Critics made the point that a Judge who is at the mercy of the Senate does not enjoy the freedom from political pressures that a member of the bench is supposed to have. For unlike one who is serving under a lifetime appoint-

[12] The Warren appointment was also pleasing to two Californians: Mr. Eisenhower's Vice President, Richard M. Nixon, and the Senate Republican Leader, William F. Knowland, both of whom rejoiced at the departure of an old rival from the political arena.

ment, he knows that each of his decisions can later be subjected to the most minute scrutiny by Senators in a position to block his permanent appointment.[13]

Whatever logic there might have been behind this criticism, Mr. Eisenhower was persuaded by an important argument on the other side. Even under ordinary circumstances, it is undesirable to compel the Supreme Court to operate without its full complement, for eight Justices may split evenly in some of their votes and thus prevent authoritative action by the highest court in the land.[14] With the time rapidly approaching for the argument in the School Segregation Cases, the circumstances were anything but ordinary, and the Court needed a Chief Justice.

In a telephone call to Sacramento, President Eisenhower told Governor Warren that he was about to be named Chief Justice of the United States. Warren, he said, should arrange to be in Washington the following Monday morning, prepared to take up the duties of the Chief Justice, for it was important that all members of the Court be present from the very beginning of the term during which the decision in the School Segregation Cases would be rendered.

Warren remembers the consternation he felt at the chaotic prospect before him. He would have to turn over the state administration of California to his successor, move his family to Washington, and assume the overwhelming responsibilities that had suddenly been thrust upon him—all in a matter of days. But the President's request for immediate action had to be honored, and precisely at noon on Monday Earl Warren stood in the Supreme Court chamber, and under his recess appointment by the President, took the oath as Chief Justice of the United States.

[13] The subject is discussed by Louis S. Loeb in a committee print of the House Committee on the Judiciary, "Recess Appointments of Federal Judges," 86th Congress, 1st Session, January, 1959.

[14] In such an instance, the Supreme Court merely announces that the decision of the lower court is affirmed. No opinion is written, and no indication is provided as to how individual Justices voted.

Senatorial Discourtesy

It was generally expected that, as soon as Congress reconvened, Warren's uncomfortable interim status would be terminated by swift Senate confirmation of his nomination. But that was not to be. The cantankerous Senator William Langer (R., N. Dak.), who was chairman of the subcommittee in charge of the preliminary screening of the nominee, had long chafed at the fact that more men from his state were not appointed to high positions in the Federal Government. Any non-North Dakotan, including Earl Warren, was fair game to the Senator.

On this occasion, Langer brushed aside the argument that it was unbecoming to subject a sitting Chief Justice to a senatorial inquisition, and conducted protracted hearings, questioning not only Warren's professional qualifications but his character as well. It was a long time before he even allowed the subcommittee to vote on the nomination, and then he insisted on reiterating a series of accusations that had been made against Warren in the course of the hearings. Thus dignified were charges centering around the contention that Warren had been involved with a lobbyist for liquor interests, and also complaints that a man with no judicial experience had been picked to preside over the Supreme Court.[15] But

[15] Lack of prior judicial experience has often provided Congressmen with a convenient stick with which to beat those Supreme Court Justices who had never before sat on the bench. There is by no means unanimity, however, about the desirability of selecting Supreme Court Justices from the lower courts. The argument, in fact, has even been made that judicial experience is a handicap, and that constitutional adjudication is more congenial to men with breadth of experience and depth of philosophical insight than to those whose lives have been spent merely in applying the legal principles laid down by others. Justice Frankfurter has noted that many outstanding members of the Supreme Court have had no apprenticeship at all on any other court: "[T]he correlation between prior judicial experience and fitness for the functions of the Supreme Court is zero. The significance of the greatest among the Justices who had had such experience, Holmes and Cardozo, derived not from that judicial experience but from the fact that they were Holmes and Cardozo. They

Langer did not actually vote against Warren, and the sub-committee recommended confirmation unanimously. On the full Judiciary Committee, there was opposition from only three of the fifteen members who voted.[16] When the nomination reached the Senate floor, none of the committee members who had expressed reservations about Warren carried their opposition to the point of voting against him. On March 1, 1954, the nomination was confirmed, and a presidential commission was issued the next day.

When the reargument of the School Segregation Cases took place, however, Warren was still presiding as Chief Justice under his recess appointment. Only one week earlier, on the opening day of the new term, he had been sworn in. According to custom, two separate oaths were used. Shortly before the public session of the Court began, he and his new colleagues gathered in the conference room, and Justice Black, as senior Associate Justice, administered the first of these, the "constitutional oath." Then at noon the members of the Court mounted the bench, with Mr. Warren taking a place near the Clerk's desk. After the Crier had intoned the traditional formula, Justice Black announced the appointment of Mr. Warren. The Clerk of the Court read the Commission issued by the President and also administered the second oath, the "judicial oath," and the new Chief Justice was then escorted to his seat in the center of the bench.

An Opinion Monday

The following Monday, with Warren sitting as Chief Justice, the Court assembled for the reargument of the school cases. After the admissions to the bar, it was time for deci-

---

were thinkers, and more particularly legal philosophers." Felix Frankfurter, "The Supreme Court in the Mirror of Justices," *University of Pennsylvania Law Review*, Vol. 105 (April, 1957), p. 795.

[16] The three who opposed confirmation were all Democrats: James O. Eastland of Mississippi, Olin Johnston of South Carolina, and Harley M. Kilgore of West Virginia.

sions to be announced. The subjects covered by the decided cases demonstrated the almost incredible variety of matters that come before the highest court in the land.

In the first of these cases, the question was whether the owner of a ship was responsible for injuries suffered by a carpenter who had been working on the vessel while it was in berth. How had such a routine controversy found its way to the Supreme Court? The case was within federal jurisdiction because the carpenter and the ship owner were citizens of different states, and the Supreme Court had granted Certiorari to review a decision rendered by the Court of Appeals.[17] The second case involved a suit to recover damages against a brokerage firm that had misrepresented securities it was selling. A federal law establishes procedures for dealing with such misrepresentation, but the Court of Appeals had split in adjudicating a fine legal point in the case and the Supreme Court had decided to take jurisdiction.[18] Then came the first criminal case of the day, in which the question was whether a Federal District Court had erred in dismissing indictments for violation of a federal law requiring dealers in gambling devices to report to the Attorney General the location of their businesses and all their sales and deliveries as well.[19] The fourth and last of the cases raised the question of whether an employer had committed an unfair labor practice under the Taft-Hartley Act in discharging certain employees. The National Labor Relations Board (NLRB) had sustained the employer's action, and its ruling had been upheld by the Court of Appeals for the District of Columbia Circuit, which can be asked to review actions by regulatory agencies.[20]

Interestingly enough, the Justices had not been able to achieve unanimity in any one of the four cases decided. Once they split 7-2, twice their vote was 6-3, and in the remaining case—the one concerned with the gambling devices—the divi-

---

[17] *Pope & Talbot, Inc.* v. *Hawn*, 346 U.S. 406 (1953).
[18] *Wilko* v. *Swan*, 346 U.S. 427 (1953).
[19] *United States* v. *Gambling Devices*, 346 U.S. 441 (1953).
[20] *Labor Board* v. *Electrical Workers*, 346 U.S. 464 (1953).

sion was 5-4. Moreover, even the bare majority of five in that last case could not get together on a single opinion. Thus Justice Jackson could only announce "the judgment of the Court," not "the opinion of the Court," and the opinion that he *did* announce was designated merely as "an opinion in which Mr. Justice Frankfurter and Mr. Justice Minton join." Because it did not have the endorsement of a majority of the Justices, it was not to be interpreted as providing authoritative guidelines to lower courts that might have to deal with the very same issues in other cases.

It was evident from the absence of unanimous decision that the Court before which the reargument in the school cases would take place was deeply divided. Whenever a new Chief Justice takes up the reins, there is hope that perhaps he can mass a united Court, for 5-4 votes are hardly calculated to enhance public acceptance of judicial decisions. If the decisions handed down on December 7, 1954, were any indication, Warren's work was cut out for him.

Reargument

At 1:05 P.M., the argument in the school cases began. The new Chief Justice announced: "No. 2, *Harry Briggs, Jr.,* et al. v. *R. W. Elliott* et al." The Clerk of the Court reported: "Counsel are present." Spottswood Robinson, the NAACP attorney who had also participated in the 1952 argument, was the first to speak and was allowed to proceed without interruption for almost thirty minutes. With respect to the questions which had been asked by the Court, he took the position that the historical materials indicated not only an intention to erase segregation generally but also a specific desire to forbid it in the public schools. When the Fourteenth Amendment was before the House, he argued, a Congressman from New Jersey had announced his opposition to it precisely *because* he understood that it would ban segregated schools.

Justice Frankfurter, who had said not a word for half an

hour, could contain himself no longer. "Mr. Robinson," he asked, "what attitude do you think the Court is called upon to manage, what weight is to be given, or how is it ever to deal with individual utterances of this, that, or other Congressmen or Senators?" Frankfurter was making a telling point, for traditionally the method for ascertaining the congressional intent is to refer back to documents such as committee reports and statements of floor managers, not to comments made by members who had no special responsibility for the legislation. But Robinson insisted that there are occasions when it is unwise to disregard statements by individual Congressmen. This was his reasoning:

> So far as the statement standing alone is concerned, I would attribute no value to it, but when a man makes that statement, is joined in it by others, and is not disputed by anyone, we have a general understanding demonstrated by the overall statements.

The answer did not satisfy Frankfurter. It seemed obvious to him that the Congressman, in saying that the Amendment would prohibit school segregation, might just have been using an old debater's trick: placing the most extreme interpretation on a proposal in order to persuade others to oppose it. There was no reason, he insisted, to trust the interpretation that had been placed on the Fourteenth Amendment by one who was campaigning for its defeat. Nor did he attach importance to the fact that no proponent of the Fourteenth Amendment had taken the floor to challenge that particular interpretation. "What does silence mean?" he asked rhetorically.

When Robinson had finished his discussion of the Fourteenth Amendment's history, it fell to Thurgood Marshall, the chief lawyer for the NAACP, to pick up where the other lawyer had left off and deal with the non-historical questions that the Court had asked. Comments from the bench indicated that the Justices were most interested in Marshall's confident assertion that they did have the power, under the Fourteenth Amendment, to abolish public school segregation through judicial action. The most skeptical reaction came from Justice Jackson, who was an adherent of the Frankfurter doctrine of "judicial restraint." Jackson said he considered it highly significant that Congress, in spite of the Fourteenth Amendment, had never felt constrained to eliminate the color line from public education by means of legislation. In the absence of legislative action, he told Marshall, there was serious doubt in his mind about the propriety of judicial action.

Marshall's answer was to insist that the Fourteenth Amendment was not intended to withhold from the courts the power to interpret and apply its provisions regardless of whether or not Congress chose to exercise *its* powers. There was thus no reason why the judiciary should be deterred by the failure of Congress to act. Quite the contrary, the fact that Congress had not legislated made it all the more important that the door not be slammed shut in the face of aggrieved individuals seeking *judicial* vindication of their rights. As Marshall saw it, the power to interpret the Constitution always remains in the hands of the courts, and in the cases being argued this meant that the Justices were free to apply the principles of the Fourteenth Amendment unhesitatingly to school segregation.

Southern History

After Marshall had completed his presentation, the Southern states had their turn. Once again it was John W. Davis who spoke for South Carolina. His study of the historical evidence, he announced, had convinced him that "the Congress which submitted, and the state legislatures which ratified, the Fourteenth Amendment did not contemplate and did not understand that it would abolish segregation in public schools . . . ." That being so, he said, the Negroes' case amounted to nothing more substantial than an exercise in sociological analysis. And even in those terms the advice given to the Court by the NAACP lawyers had little to recommend it, for there was no reason to believe either that Negro children would be happier in interracial schools or that they would do better work. As far as the question of judicial power was concerned, the lawyer argued that the "separate but equal" principle had been "so often announced, so confidently relied upon, [and] so long continued" that it was no longer subject to re-evaluation by the Court.

There was still time on the opening day of the argument for a second lawyer, T. Justin Moore, to continue the presentation of the case for the South. Moore, who represented Virginia in the litigation, was urged by Justice Frankfurter to give the Court his views on the kind of decree that should be issued if the decision was to abolish segregation. The lawyer appeared upset at the mere thought that things might come to such a pass. "It really distresses me to face that question," he told Frankfurter. "About all I can say is we feel the courts should be given the broadest possible discretion to act along reasonable lines . . . . The parties certainly should be allowed to present a plan rather than for the Court to just hand down a plan."

The position of Virginia was further elaborated the next day by the state's Attorney General, J. Lindsay Almond. According to Almond, the NAACP lawyers were really asking the Court

> to make a decision contrary to the spirit, the intent, and purpose of the Fourteenth Amendment. They are asking you to amend the Constitution of the United States. . . . They are asking you to disturb and tear down the principle . . . enunciated so clearly in 1896 in *Plessy* v. *Ferguson*. . . . They are asking you to disturb the unfolding evolutionary process of education. . . .

Moreover, said Almond, if the Court declared segregation unconstitutional, administrative problems of unmanageable proportions would confront Virginia, to the extent that the state might even have to consider repealing its compulsory attendance law. The hint that Virginia might try to circumvent an adverse decision was, of course, not lost on the Justices.[21]

The Government's Turn

During the remainder of the three-day argument, eight other attorneys came before the bench to speak in behalf of the different parties in the five law suits. Assistant Attorney General Rankin presented the views of the United States Government as *amicus curiae*. There was great interest in what he would have to say, for the Government's brief had raised more questions than it had answered. So equivocal had the brief been that Justice Douglas said he was unable to ascertain whether the Government had actually taken a position on the merits of the constitutional controversy. Rankin replied that it had. " . . . It is the position of the Department of Justice," he said, "that segregation in public schools cannot be maintained under the Fourteenth Amendment. . . ." Douglas appeared satisfied. "I just wanted to clear up that

[21] As it turned out, Almond himself later became Governor of Virginia, and it was largely up to him to decide how the state should respond to the school desegregation decree issued by the Supreme Court. Although he had pledged during his campaign to carry out a policy of "massive resistance," once in office he proved to be far from intransigent when it became evident that some degree of school desegregation was inevitable. His willingness to compromise was not appreciated by Harry F. Byrd, who was both the senior Senator from Virginia and the head of the Democratic machine of the state, and when President Kennedy selected Almond for a seat on the United States Court of Customs and Patent Appeals, Byrd used his influence with the Southern members of the Senate Judiciary Committee to block the nomination. After standing in Almond's way for more than a year, Byrd finally decided that his former friend had been punished enough, and the nomination was allowed to go through. Earlier, Byrd had dissuaded President Kennedy from naming Almond to a more desirable district judgeship by threatening to invoke "senatorial courtesy" if the nomination were made. The establishment of Virginia's policy on implementation of the Supreme Court's decision is described in Robbin L. Gates, *The Making of Massive Resistance: Virginia's Politics of Public School Desegregation, 1954–1956* (Chapel Hill: University of North Carolina Press, 1964).

confusion in my mind," he said.

Rankin took note of the criticism that had been leveled at the Government for the way in which it had presented the historical evidence. He would by no means concede that he and his associates in the Department of Justice owed an apology either "to your Honors or to the country" for seeming to straddle the fence. Nothing in the Government's brief, he insisted, had been intended to convey the impression that the legislative history of the Fourteenth Amendment failed to cast light on the school question. Quite the reverse, the history was extremely important because it showed that the framers of the Amendment had never said a single word to indicate that they wanted to *preserve* school segregation. And this was significant because it meant that the Court was completely free to strike down separate schools in accordance with the sweeping terms of the Amendment.

The Assistant Attorney General went further than that, making a frontal attack on the theory that the right to non-discriminatory treatment could only be vindicated by Congress and not by the Court. Agreeing with the NAACP, he said: "The whole concept of constitutional law is that constitutional rights are not to be subject to the political forum, which changes from time to time."

But the position of the Government's lawyer was far less satisfactory to the NAACP on the question of how an anti-segregation decision could best be implemented. Rankin said that the emphasis should be on the development of local solutions, not the imposition of one national timetable. School officials in each area should be allowed to explain any peculiar problems in their jurisdiction to a Federal District judge, and if time was really needed the judge could grant it as long as the local authorities were really trying to liquidate segregated schools.

Justice Jackson asked Rankin to be specific about the kind of problems that could justify a request for more time. The lawyer replied that he was thinking only of administrative difficulties, such as the inadequacy of buildings or transportation facilities. The District Courts, he said, should be careful to distinguish between such legitimate reasons for delay and any "deliberate attempt to evade the judgment of this Court . . . . "

A Moot Question

The attorney who followed Rankin to the lectern, Robert L. Carter of the NAACP, was confronted with a knotty technical problem. A few seconds after he began his argument in the Topeka case, he was interrupted by Justice Frankfurter. "Is your case moot, Mr. Carter?" Frankfurter asked. The lawyer's reply provoked laughter in the courtroom. "I hoped that I would get a little further into the argument before that question was asked," he said.

What Frankfurter was driving at was that possibly a genuine controversy no longer existed in the Kansas case. After all, two schools in Topeka had already been desegregated, and a plan was in operation to eliminate separate schools entirely. One could argue that, under these circumstances, only hypothetical questions were being presented, not questions arising out of an actual clash between the two parties, and traditionally the judiciary remains aloof from such cases since its jurisdiction is limited by the Constitution to flesh-and-blood controversies.

But was the Kansas case really moot? Only one of *his* clients, Carter noted, had been admitted to a white school. Moreover, although the local board of education had been cooperative in instituting a desegregation plan, the state of Kansas continued to deny adamantly that any constitutional rights of the Negro children had been violated.

The argument over mootness went on when the Assistant Attorney General of Kansas, Paul E. Wilson, made his presentation to the Court. Wilson said he agreed with Carter that a real, not a hypothetical, case still existed. This point was promptly challenged by several of the Justices, with

Frankfurter in the forefront. At first Chief Justice Warren suffered in silence while Frankfurter interrupted the lawyer over and over again, but his patience was finally exhausted. "I think when both parties to the action feel that there is a controversy, and invited the Attorney General to be here and answer these questions, I, for one, would like to hear the argument," he said icily.[22]

If at times a chill descended over the courtroom, there were also some light moments. When the lawyer for Kansas referred to his counterpart from Virginia as "Judge Moore" instead of plain "Mr. Moore," he was corrected. But in the presence of nine *Judges* he somehow could not bring himself to apologize for his mistake, lest the apology appear to imply that to be called a judge was an insult. "I am not sure whether it is proper to apologize under the circumstances or not," he said with mock hesitation, and the Justices dissolved in laughter.

Upon the conclusion of the argument over Kansas, the Court started on the case that questioned the maintenance of segregated public schools by the District of Columbia. Although the Fourteenth Amendment does not apply in the nation's capital, it was referred to frequently. The lawyer for the District placed great emphasis on the fact that the very same Congress which had passed the Amendment had also legislated repeatedly for the support of segregated schools in Washington, thus signifying that it saw no incompatability between school segregation and the "due process of law" that had to be observed by both the states and the Federal Government. Counsel for the NAACP, however, insisted that Con-

[22] Sharp words are often exchanged by the Justices in open court. Chief Justice Warren's implied rebuke of Justice Frankfurter during the argument in the Topeka case was only one in a long series of such incidents involving the two men. Nor were Warren and Frankfurter the only Justices who traded caustic comments. On one occasion, Justice Douglas leveled a biting attack on his old friend, Justice Black. Referring to a lengthy opinion by Black, Douglas said that his colleague had really written not a judicial analysis but rather a kind of congressional committee report, and that the purpose of its excess verbiage was to conceal a dearth of valid arguments.

gress had never intended to approve racial segregation for the city of Washington. The funds it had appropriated for Negro schools merely reflected a realization that the freedmen could not generally afford to attend the private schools where white children were enrolled.

In the District of Columbia case, as well as the cases from South Carolina, Virginia, and Kansas, the NAACP attorneys had the opportunity to present their arguments first, because in each instance it was the Negroes who had persuaded the Supreme Court to review a decision unfavorable to them. But in the final case that was heard, the one from Delaware, the situation was reversed. Since the Negroes had won in Delaware, both in the Court of Chancery and in the State Supreme Court, the state was the appellant and therefore entitled to begin the arguments.

It did so in the person of its Attorney General, Joseph Donald Craven. There was really not much for Craven to add to what had already been said on behalf of Kansas, South Carolina, and Virginia. He could not even enumerate the obstacles that allegedly would have to be surmounted in order to implement any adverse decision, for school desegregation in his state was already well under way, in accordance with a decree of the Delaware Supreme Court.

Nevertheless, the Negro appellees in Delaware were not entirely satisfied with the victory they had won in the lower courts. For the chancellor's ruling, which the State Supreme Court had affirmed, was that the Negro children in Newcastle County would have to be admitted to the white schools only because the segregated facilities that had been provided for them could not match those available to whites. This ruling fell far short of a finding that segregated treatment constituted unequal treatment in and of itself, and it was this finding that the NAACP lawyer, Jack Greenberg, argued for in the Supreme Court. Greenberg, who was later to succeed Thurgood Marshall in his NAACP position, said that until there was a flat invalidation of segregated schools the Negro children would remain "under a cloud" and would not be "like the rest of the students in the school."

It was 2:42 P.M. on December 9, 1953, when the oral argument in the Delaware case came to an end. The Justices had listened to more than ten hours of arguments and counter-arguments in the five cases. Now the decision that they had once deferred would finally have to be made.

7. Decision Day

More than five months elapsed before the Supreme Court announced its decision. Such a lengthy period of parturition is not unusual in a difficult case, for a majority cannot be mustered overnight in support of an opinion explaining why a certain action has been taken.

Not too many days after the argument was held, the Justices assembled in the privacy of their conference room to discuss the five segregation cases.[1] The Chief Justice initiated the discussion with a statement of his own views on how the case should be decided. After that, the senior Associate Justice, Hugo Black, had his turn to speak, and then the privilege of the floor passed in turn to each of the other Associate Justices in order of seniority. Each took as much time as he liked, and in accordance with custom, interruptions were rare. Sherman Minton, the junior Justice, was the last to be given the floor for his opening statement before the conference shifted gears and began the far less formal process of back-and-forth discussion of the various issues involved. When in time the Justices were ready to vote, Minton had the consolation of being the first to be called on. This procedure accorded with the amiable custom that is supposed to encourage the newer members of the Court to vote their own convictions instead

[1] The regular conference day, which used to be Saturday, is now Friday. The Court made the change in 1955.

of being swayed unduly by their senior colleagues. Accordingly, the next Justice to vote was the one who was senior only to Minton, and so on up the line, with Justice Black casting the penultimate vote and Chief Justice Warren voting last. As each vote was announced, Warren recorded it in his docket book.

As the votes were tallied, history was being written. When it was all over, the Court had struck down school segregation as incompatible with the Constitution of the United States.

The decision that was reached, however, was only tentative, for any Justice may reconsider his vote and change sides up to the very moment when a final decision is publicly announced. But it is on the basis of the tentative decision that the Chief Justice performs one of his most important functions: determining who will write the opinion explaining the rationale of the Court's action.

Assignment Power

Actually, the Chief Justice is sometimes deprived of the opportunity to exercise this power. That happens on the frequent occasions when he finds himself in the minority in a particular case. In such an event, with the Chief Justice disagreeing with a majority of his colleagues, the assignment power passes to the senior Associate Justice on the predominant side. Similarly, it has long been the policy for the Chief Justice to step aside and allow a member who has just joined the Court to pick for himself the case in which he will write his maiden opinion. But except for these instances it is for the Chief Justice to decide who shall prepare the various Opinions of the Court. His decisions are communicated to the other Justices by means of an "assignment list" that he circulates a few days after the conference is held.

During the early years of the Supreme Court's history, no assignment of opinions was necessary. In the tradition of the English courts, each Justice would write up a statement of his own views, and there would be as many opinions as there were Justices. But when John Marshall took office as Chief Justice in 1801, he came to feel strongly that the Court would be more authoritative and would command greater respect if it could manage to speak with a single voice. At his behest, each case thereafter resulted in an Opinion of the Court, written by him or by one of his colleagues but also endorsed by the others.[2] Marshall's ideal was unanimity, and he strove mightily—and usually successfully—to achieve it, even at the cost of compromising his own individual views in certain cases.[3]

Today a Chief Justice will assign no more opinions to himself than he will to any of his colleagues. His power to decide who shall speak in a particular case, however, is of substantive significance. By selecting one Justice rather than another to write a given opinion, he is predetermining, at least to an extent, the content of the opinion. This is so not only because the Justices' general philosophical positions are a matter of record, but also because their views on the specific case have been exposed at the conference.

Yet the significance of this point should not be overstated, for in practical terms the Chief Justice does not really possess absolute discretion. He must take certain objective factors into account. If, for example, he assigns a case to a Justice who can be expected to write an opinion in broad and sweeping terms, the likelihood that there will be quick public acceptance of the Court's action may be considerably diminished. It may in fact seem politic to have the opinion prepared and announced by a man whose views are generally congenial to the very segment of the community that will be adversely affected

[2] Jefferson was irate at Marshall for the reform he had instituted. As he saw it, opinions were being "huddled up in conclaves, perhaps by a majority of one, delivered as if unanimous, and with the silent acquiescence of lazy or timid associates, by a crafty Chief Judge, who sophisticates the law to his own mind, by the turn of his own reasoning."

[3] See William Winslow Crosskey, "John Marshall," in Allison Dunham and Philip B. Kurland, eds., *Mr. Justice* (Chicago: University of Chicago Press, 1964), p. 7.

by the decision.[4] Moreover, an unnecessarily broad opinion is likely to encourage the proliferation of concurrences and dissents; it may even persuade some of the Justices who stood originally with the majority to switch their position. This change could conceivably nullify the earlier action of the conference and result in deciding the case the other way.

There is, however, another reason why the Chief Justice's assignment power is important. By turning over the responsibility for an opinion to a colleague who voted with him only hesitantly and with his mind not really quite made up, he makes it far less likely that the man will undergo a change of heart and cross over to the other side. Furthermore, a new member of the Court who has himself written and announced the opinion in a controversial case will later find it harder to abandon the law enunciated in the case than if he had merely gone along passively with an opinion written by a senior colleague.

The Chief Justice must also bear in mind certain mundane considerations. For example, he has to try to distribute the work load evenly. And while he may want to take advantage of a senior Justice's expertise in a difficult area of the law (such as taxation or patents), he must balance this wish against the desirability of giving a junior member of the Court the chance to become familiar with a subject that is quite new to him.

Occasionally a personal and even sentimental factor may determine the assignment of an opinion. When, for example, the Court voted in 1963 to repudiate a ruling of twenty-two years earlier and uphold the unconditional right to counsel in all criminal trials, the writing of the opinion was assigned quite naturally to Justice Black, for he had filed a passionate dissent in the previous case and had never softened his criticism in the intervening years.[5]

---

[4] Henry J. Abraham, *The Judicial Process* (New York: Oxford University Press, 1962), pp. 186–88.

[5] *Gideon* v. *Wainwright*, 372 U.S. 335 (1963), overruling *Betts* v. *Brady*, 316 U.S. 455 (1942).

Dissenting Opinions

No formal procedure is used for assigning the writing of a dissenting opinion when the Court is split. The members who find themselves outvoted simply get together and decide who should be responsible for producing an opinion. Their aim is to preserve their views for the record in the hope that some day, with new Justices on the Court or with a different atmosphere prevailing, these views may be translated into law.

But the dissenters may also have a more immediate hope in mind: the possibility that their opinion may prove persuasive to one or more of the Justices who voted originally on the other side.[6] The result of such a shift, of course, may be that the minority will suddenly be converted into a majority. As one of the Justices has written, "It is a common experience that dissents change votes, even enough votes to become the majority." The Justice added unhappily: "I have had to convert more than one of my proposed majority opinions into a dissent before the final decision was announced."[7]

In most instances, dissenting opinions make better reading than majority opinions, for the latter suffer from the fact that they are essentially collaborative efforts. Although one man does write the first draft of what is to become the "Opinion of the Court," he circulates this version among the other Justices, who are typically anything but reticent in their comments. The "returns" that they send back may contain proposals for all sorts of additions, deletions, and revisions of the draft opinion.

[6] Occasionally one of the Justices voting with the majority announces at the conference that he will reserve final judgment pending circulation of the dissent. The Foundation of the Federal Bar Association, *Equal Justice Under Law* (Washington, 1965), p. 141.

[7] It may, of course, go the other way. The same Justice added that he had also had "the more satisfying experience of rewriting a dissent as a majority opinion for the Court." William J. Brennan, "Inside View of the High Court," *The New York Times Magazine,* October 6, 1963, p. 102.

The author of the draft will hesitate to rebuff even the most unwelcome suggestion, for he knows that otherwise some of his brethren may decide to write up formal statements of their own individual views and file these as "concurring opinions." Above all he wants to retain the support of at least five Justices for his draft so that it will be recognized as the authoritative "Opinion of the Court." As a consequence, he tends to be (in the words of Justice Benjamin N. Cardozo) "cautious, timid, fearful of the vivid word, the heightened phrase." Not so the dissenter: "For the moment he is the gladiator making a last stand against the lion." [8]

In all likelihood, Chief Justice Warren had no trouble deciding who should write the opinion that would seal the fate of school segregation and possibly all other types of segregation as well. Such a momentous pronouncement would come most fittingly from the Chief Justice of the United States. At the same time, it would help facilitate public acceptance of the decision if the Court could be unanimous in its judgment. Dissenting opinions would provide a ready rallying point for opponents of the decision, and separate concurring opinions might even do damage by disclosing disagreement on the precise constitutional basis of the Court's action.

Because it was so important to attain unanimity, an extraordinary process of consultation and negotiation was initiated. Even members of the Court who were far from enthusiastic about a judicial invalidation of segregated schools cooperated in the attempt to forge a reasonable compromise around which a unanimous Court could be assembled. But all this took time. Weeks stretched into months, winter yielded to spring, and public suspense mounted as to what the Court would do. Yet the Justices were in no hurry. Time after time a new opinion was drafted and sent to the "leak-proof" shop that the Government Printing Office maintains in the basement of the Court building. Every draft was circulated to all nine Justices for their comments. Sometimes just a sentence or two

[8] Quoted by Justice Clark in an address to the University of Minnesota Law School Alumni Association, April 13, 1959.

would be scribbled on the draft and returned to the author. At other times, a comprehensive critique would be prepared.

Finally the entire elaborate process of draft and counter-draft was concluded, and at the conference on Saturday, May 15, 1954, Chief Justice Warren announced to his colleagues that the opinion in the school cases was ready to be handed down on the following Monday.

Admissions to the Bar

When the Justices ascended the bench at noon on Monday, May 17, 1954, a time-consuming formality had to be observed before the reading of opinions could begin: the admission of lawyers to the Supreme Court Bar. In the course of the typical year, nearly 3,000 lawyers appear in Court to have their admission moved by others who are already members. On this particular day, 118 were admitted.[9] Some had their names put forth by well-known public figures. Former Secretary of State Dean G. Acheson was there to present his son, David C. Acheson, and a number of members of Congress were in attendance to move other admissions. All of them adhered closely to the traditional formula: "Mr. Chief Justice, I have the honor to move the admission of _____ of the Bar of the State of _____. I am satisfied that he possesses the necessary qualifications." The "necessary qualifications" are minimal: membership in the Bar of the highest court of a jurisdiction for at least three years, written endorsement by two members of the Supreme Court Bar, and the payment of a twenty-five-dollar fee.[10]

The fee used to be more important than it is today. Until a few years ago, Congress appropriated no money at all for

[9] Monday always drew a large number of applicants for admission, because that was "Opinion Day," the high point of the Supreme Court week, when decisions were announced. In 1965, however, this system was abandoned, and now opinions are read on other days, too.

[10] Rules 5 and 52 of the *Rules of the Supreme Court,* 346 U.S. 953 and 1002 (1954).

the maintenance of the Supreme Court Clerk's Office. Accordingly, all expenses of that office—the salaries of its employees, plane fare for the lawyers in *in forma pauperis* cases, and the cost of printing briefs for indigents—had to be paid for out of a "fee fund" that could fluctuate widely from one year to the next. The fund was made up of money paid to the Clerk's Office in the form of fees for the supervision of printing, docketing fees, and fees for admission to the Supreme Court Bar. Now Congress has finally acted to provide the Clerk's Office with its own annual appropriation, so since 1963 the money realized through fees has been turned over to the United States Treasury.

On that historic Monday in 1954, the cut-and-dried admission formula was recited over and over again, and the Clerk administered the oath to the new members of the Supreme Court Bar in groups of thirty or so.[11] It was then time for opinions to be announced.[12] Spectators in the courtroom could have no inkling of whether or not the school opinions would be handed down that day, though some thought it might be

[11] Only a small minority of the lawyers admitted each year ever get to argue a case in the Supreme Court. Moreover, when a lawyer who is not a member of the Supreme Court Bar is retained to argue a case, a simple procedure is available for him to be admitted *pro hac vice* (just for this one time). All it takes is a motion by a member of the Bar (Rule 6 of the *Rules of the Supreme Court*, 346 U.S. 953–54 [1954]). In the nineteenth century, the Supreme Court Bar was a more prestigious group than today. Its members, who were specialists in Supreme Court practice, would handle litigation for other lawyers who were too far from Washington even to think of arguing their own cases in the Supreme Court.

[12] Before Vinson became Chief Justice, the reverse order was followed, and admissions to the Bar did not come until after opinions had been read. That meant that for the presentation of opinions the Court would have what one writer referred to as "a captive audience of prominence"—particularly the Members of Congress who were waiting to move the admission of constituents. When Vinson, who had been a member of the House, was appointed to the Court, he had the system changed, in order to avoid wasting the time of congressmen. Doubtless no objection came from either Justices Black or Burton, for both of them had once served in the Senate and were thus cognizant of the problem. John P. Frank, *Marble Palace: The Supreme Court in American Life* (New York: Knopf, 1958), p. 122.

significant that Justice Jackson had left a sickbed in order to be present.[13]

According to custom, when the newest member of the Court has an opinion to deliver, he is the first to be recognized by the Chief Justice, and then, in reverse seniority order, come the other members of the Court who have opinions to announce. The junior Justice, Sherman Minton, had none to present that day, so Chief Justice Warren turned to the next junior Justice, Tom Clark, and with a nod of his head signaled to him that he could now begin. Clark's case dealt with a question of monopolistic practices in the sale of milk in Chicago.[14] After that came Justice Douglas: first, with a decision that the Government was not entitled to collect an indemnity from a federal employee who had been guilty of negligence,[15] and then with one involving the picketing of retail stores by a bakery-workers' union.[16] Since no other Associate Justice had any opinion to deliver, it was the turn of the Chief Justice, whose opinions are always the last to be presented. "I have for announcement," Warren began, "the judgment and opinion of the Court in No. 1, *Brown* et al. v. *Board of Education of Topeka* et al."

News in the Making

As Chief Justice Warren began reading the opinion, a procession of news reporters entered the courtroom, led by Banning E. Whittington, the Court's Press Officer. They had been alerted just moments earlier that this was to be the big day and had lost no time following Whittington as he left the press room and climbed the long flight of marble stairs to the main floor of the building, where the courtroom is situated.

For most of the reporters, such a visit to the courtroom is made only infrequently. Instead, decision days are spent

13 Jackson died less than five months later.
14 *United States* v. *Borden Company,* 347 U.S. 514 (1954).
15 *United States* v. *Gilman,* 347 U.S. 507 (1954).
16 *Capital Service, Inc.* v. *Labor Board,* 347 U.S. 501 (1954).

in the press room. Not only are typewriters and telephones available there, but even more important, there is faster access to opinions. Sitting in the courtroom while decisions are being announced can be a frustrating experience for a reporter with an early deadline, because when a Justice launches into the reading of an opinion he may give no immediate indication of how the Court has decided the case. The first part of the document he reads may describe the route by which the case reached the Court and recite the relevant facts, and the rest of the opinion may be written in something of an O. Henry style, keeping the reporter waiting until the very last paragraph for the "surprise ending." [17]

In the press room, the situation is entirely different. Only seconds after the reading of an opinion begins, a number identifying the case is received by the Court's Press Officer through a pneumatic tube device connecting the courtroom and the press room. Immediately the Press Officer opens a safe in which earlier that morning he stored the opinions due to be released, and distributes copies to the waiting reporters so that they can begin to file their stories without delay.

But on this day the usual routine was not observed. As soon as the Press Officer learned from a note in the pneumatic tube that the school cases were due in a matter of seconds, he announced to the waiting reporters that the reading of the Segregation Decisions was about to begin in the courtroom. "You will get the opinions later on," he said. "Follow me." He pulled on his coat and started toward the courtroom with perhaps thirty newsmen right behind him.

[17] Five reporters in the courtroom, however, have no such problems. These are the representatives of the two major wire services (Associated Press and United Press International) and of *The New York Times, Baltimore Sun,* and *Washington Post.* Unlike their colleagues who are seated in the regular press section, these five, who cover the Court regularly, have individual desks that are even closer to the bench than the lectern used by the lawyers during oral argument. As soon as the reading of an opinion begins, they receive proof copies from the boys who serve as pages in the Court, and can scan these quickly to ascertain which way the decision has gone.

"Inherently Unequal"

Warren was in the process of reading his opinion as the reporters streamed into the courtroom. He had begun by explaining how the four cases involving segregation in Southern states had reached the Supreme Court. Now he continued with a discussion of the issue raised by the lawyers for the Negro children. "The plaintiffs contend," he said, "that segregated public schools are not 'equal' and cannot be made 'equal,' and that hence they are deprived of the equal protection of the laws." How much light was cast on the problem by the history of the Fourteenth Amendment, which had been studied so meticulously in the briefs? The Court's answer was succinct: ". . . Not enough to resolve the problem with which we are faced." At best, it said, the historical data was inconclusive, perhaps because public education in the South was not sufficiently advanced in their day for the framers of the Fourteenth Amendment to be very much concerned with it.

But the status of public education had changed drastically since then, Warren pointed out. "Today," he said, "education is perhaps the most important function of state and local governments"—so important that "in these days, it is doubtful that any child may reasonably be expected to succeed in life if he is denied the opportunity of an education."

Under these circumstances, said the Chief Justice, the Court had come to this conclusion: Where a state has undertaken to provide the opportunity of an education to its citizens, that opportunity is "a right which must be made available to all on equal terms." That having been decided, only one question remained: "Does segregation of children in public schools solely on the basis of race, even though the physical facilities and other 'tangible' factors may be equal, deprive the children of the minority group of equal educational opportunities?" The Court's answer was unequivocal: "We believe that it does."

In deciding that segregated education subjects the Negro child to an unconstitutional discrimination, the Court was heavily influenced by the deleterious effects of classification by race. As Warren put it, "To separate [Negro children] from others of similar age and qualifications solely because of their race generates a feeling of inferiority as to their status in the community that may affect their hearts and minds in a way unlikely ever to be undone." But what about *Plessy* v. *Ferguson*, in which the Court had found in 1896 that no damage was inflicted by segregation? The answer was brief and to the point: "Whatever may have been the extent of psychological knowledge at the time of *Plessy* v. *Ferguson*, this finding [that segregation is damaging] is amply supported by modern authority. Any language in *Plessy* v. *Ferguson* contrary to this finding is rejected."

What came next was almost anticlimactic: "We conclude that in the field of public education the doctrine of 'separate but equal' has no place. Separate educational facilities are inherently unequal." [18]

On the constitutional question, then, the finding of the Court was unequivocal. But there were no immediate decrees ordering an end to school segregation in the affected areas. The Justices felt that they needed "the full assistance of the parties" in formulating decrees, for the cases presented "problems of considerable complexity." Adopting the Government's suggestion of 1952, they restored the cases to their docket and requested that further argument be held on how the constitutional decision should be implemented. The Attorney General of the United States was asked to participate again, as he had in 1953, and the attorneys general of the states with segregated public schools were also invited to appear as *amici curiae*. By accepting a role in the argument, of course, they would be lending legitimacy to the Court's ultimate decision.

[18] *Brown* v. *Board of Education,* 347 U.S. 483 (1954).

Brevity and Unanimity

From beginning ("These cases come to us from the states of Kansas, South Carolina, Virginia, and Delaware") to end ("It is so ordered"), the reading of the opinion had taken less than fifteen minutes, although the Chief Justice did not omit a single word. Including footnotes, the text occupied barely ten pages in the published version, despite the large type and wide margins favored by the Court for its opinions. For such a momentous case, the opinion was extraordinarily brief and easy to read.

Even more striking was the fact that the opinion was unanimous. Supreme Court Justices are an individualistic lot, and more often than not they are hopelessly divided on the most significant cases. But there was no dissent in the school cases, nor even a separate concurring opinion. It may be stated, however, that right up to the end Justice Reed had considered noting his disagreement with the Court's action. Whatever doubts some of the other Justices had felt had been dispelled. Frankfurter and Jackson had been won over by the Department of Justice's assurance that a moderate approach to implementation could be adopted; Minton had abandoned his opposition to school desegregation after losing a staunch ally when Chief Justice Vinson died; and about this time Clark, too, had been persuaded by the Chief Justice to go along with the majority. Officially, therefore, the vote in favor of the decision was 9 to 0.

Similar unanimity marked the decision in the District of Columbia case, which was announced immediately afterward by the Chief Justice. Since a different constitutional provision had been invoked in this case than in the four other cases, it took a separate opinion to explain the Court's resolution of the issues presented.

Fewer than 600 words were used to apply the Fifth Amendment to school segregation in the nation's capital. That

Amendment forbids any governmental action depriving an individual of life, liberty, or property without due process of law. Liberty, said the Court, "is not confined to mere freedom from bodily restraint." Rather it

> extends to the full range of conduct which the individual is free to pursue, and it cannot be restricted except for a proper governmental objective. Segregation in public education is not reasonably related to any proper governmental objective, and thus it imposes on Negro children of the District of Columbia a burden that constitutes an arbitrary deprivation of their liberty in violation of the due process clause.[19]

In these words the Court explained why the District of Columbia could no more impose segregation on Negro school children than could the states. Warren spoke of the anomaly that would have resulted if the Court, after interpreting the Fourteenth Amendment to prohibit segregated schools, had not read the same meaning into the Fifth Amendment. "In view of our decision that the Constitution prohibits the states from maintaining racially segregated public schools," he said, "it would be unthinkable that the same Constitution would impose a lesser duty on the Federal Government."

Just as it did in the four state cases, the Supreme Court postponed the issuance of a decree in the District of Columbia case to allow time for reargument on how the prohibition against school segregation should be implemented.[20]

[19] There was more than a hint here that the old "substantive due process" doctrine was being resurrected—the doctrine under which the Court, prior to 1937, had struck down dozens of laws intended to ameliorate a wide variety of social and economic evils. More than a decade after the school segregation decision, a member of the Court who was by no means a defender of "substantive due process" explained the basis on which he had understood the District of Columbia decision to rest. The decision, said Justice Black, "merely recognized what had been the understanding from the beginning of the country, an understanding shared by many of the draftsmen of the Fourteenth Amendment, that the whole Bill of Rights, including the Due Process Clause of the Fifth Amendment, was a guarantee that all persons would receive equal treatment under the law." (*Griswold* v. *Connecticut*, 381 U.S. 479, 517 [1965] [dissenting opinion].)

[20] *Bolling* v. *Sharpe*, 347 U.S. 497 (1954).

8. Conclusion: Implementing the Decision

Almost a whole year went by before the Supreme Court assembled to hear argument on implementation. Events, of course, had not stood still in the intervening months. As far as the District of Columbia was concerned, President Eisenhower announced that there was no need for any judicial order to make the Federal Government perceive its clear responsibilities. The city of Washington, he said, should set an example for the rest of the nation by abolishing segregation quickly, without any ifs, ands, or buts. Upon his urging, swift action ensued to integrate the schools of the District of Columbia, which had the largest proportion of Negroes of any major American city. There was similar action in a number of the border states, and before long, segregation had been eliminated in approximately five hundred school districts containing a quarter of a million Negro pupils.

In the Deep South, however, events were not quite as encouraging, with the Supreme Court and its members subjected to the most unrestrained kind of abuse by politicians, newspaper editors, and ministers of the gospel. This reaction, of course, was to be expected. It would have been nothing short of extraordinary if Southern whites had been able to confront the demand for a veritable revolution in their way of life without the consolation of some purple prose. What was noteworthy immediately after the 1954 decision was not the denunciation so much as the lack of outright defiance. The general attitude, in fact, was one of resignation: "They" had made an odious decision, but one had come to expect such things from the Federal Government—and there was nothing at all that could be done.

Between the time that the main decision on school segregation was announced and the time that the argument on implementation was held, a new Justice was named to the Court. To replace Justice Jackson, who died in October, 1954, President Eisenhower selected a man whose name was redolent with history. The nominee, John Marshall Harlan, was the namesake and grandson of the Justice who had been the solitary dissenter in the Plessy case of 1896, when the Court placed its stamp of approval on the "separate but equal" doctrine. Since Harlan's ancestry made him a convenient symbol of racial equality, Southern Senators dramatized their displeasure with the stand that the Court had taken by using their power to delay confirmation of the nomination. When action finally came, nine of the eleven votes cast against Harlan came from Southern Democrats.

The procrastination in the Senate accounted for the long hiatus between the May 17th decision and the arguments on implementation, for Chief Justice Warren and his colleagues did not want the enforcement problem taken up by a truncated Court. It was not until April 11, 1955, that the oral argument on implementation began.

Advice on Implementation

Due to illness, John W. Davis was unable to argue for South Carolina this time. There was, however, no shortage of legal talent in the South, and the states that participated in the oral argument were able to make their case loud and clear. The Supreme Court decree, they said, should repose primary responsibility for implementation on Federal District judges, and no obstruction should be placed in the way of a gradual approach. South Carolina argued, for example, that particularly since Clarendon County was a rural area its people needed abundant time to adjust to anything so far-reaching as school desegregation. Of the six Southern states that participated in the cases as *amici curiae,* Florida chose not to appear for the oral argument, and the other five— Arkansas, Maryland, North Carolina, Oklahoma, and Texas— did little more than plead for permission to tackle the problem at the local level.

In the view of the NAACP, the South was recommending a course of action that would preserve segregated schools indefinitely, for the District judges in the South, overwhelmingly Southern themselves, could be depended on to drag their feet.[1] Thurgood Marshall, arguing his fiftieth case in the Supreme Court, said that two things were needed at the very least: the issuance of a clear command to the district judges, and the imposition of an early deadline. Personally, of course, he and his associates saw an order for immediate and across-the-board integration as the best answer, but they doubted that the Court would be willing to go beyond what the Department of Justice had recommended, since, in the final analysis, enforcement would be in the hands of the Executive Branch. Moreover, questions from the bench indicated deep concern among the members of the Court that there might be widespread defiance of a stern decree.

The apprehension felt by the Justices was heightened when a Southern lawyer stressed that the wrong kind of decree

[1] Actual experience from 1955 to the present has indicated that in decision on school segregation the Courts of Appeals have been far more sympathetic to the Negro than the District Courts, whose members are generally hand-picked by Southern Democratic Senators and merely rubberstamped by the President. Jack W. Peltason, *58 Lonely Men: Southern Federal Judges and School Desegregation* (New York: Harcourt, Brace & World, 1961), p. 28.

Nos. 1, 2, 3, 4, 5

In the Supreme Court of the United States

OCTOBER TERM, 1954

No. 1

OLIVER BROWN, ET AL., APPELLANTS
v.
BOARD OF EDUCATION OF TOPEKA, ET AL.

No. 2

HARRY BRIGGS, JR., ET AL., APPELLANTS
v.
R. W. ELLIOTT, ET AL.

No. 3

DOROTHY E. DAVIS, ET AL., APPELLANTS
v.
COUNTY SCHOOL BOARD OF PRINCE EDWARD COUNTY, ET AL.

No. 4

SPOTTSWOOD THOMAS BOLLING, ET AL., PETITIONERS
v.
C. MELVIN SHARPE, ET AL.

No. 5

FRANCIS B. GEBHART, ET AL., PETITIONERS
v.
ETHEL LOUISE BELTON, ET AL.

BRIEF FOR THE UNITED STATES ON THE FURTHER ARGUMENT OF THE QUESTIONS OF RELIEF

HERBERT BROWNELL, Jr.,
Attorney General,
SIMON E. SOBELOFF,
Solicitor General,
J. LEE RANKIN,
Assistant Attorney General,
PHILIP ELMAN,
ALAN S. ROSENTHAL,
Special Assistants to the Attorney General,
Department of Justice, Washington 25, D. C.

The titles of all five cases are listed by the Department of Justice on the cover of its amicus *brief on implementation.*

might simply be ignored, just as Prohibition was. Marshall was enraged that a comparison was being made between the two situations. "I am shocked," he said, "that anyone would put the right of Negroes to equal participation in our system of education on a par with the right to take a drink of whiskey." A different sort of response came from one of Marshall's associates. Spottswood Robinson reminded the Justices that anyone flouting a Court decree on school segregation would put himself in contempt of Court, and the Judiciary did not lack weapons to deal with that.

By the time that the Department of Justice had its turn to argue as *amicus curiae,* the Court had already listened for almost three full days to arguments on implementation. Solicitor General Simon E. Soboloff used this fact as the basis for a little joke to introduce his presentation. "Arising to address the Court toward the end of the third day of argument in this case," he said, "it seems to me that the Court might invoke for its own protection the Eighth Amendment, which guarantees it against cruel and unusual punishment." The remark was a perfect example of courtroom humor: urbane, erudite—and not very funny.

The proposal that Soboloff presented on behalf of the Government purported to be a compromise, combining the firmness recommended by the Negroes with the gradualism on which the Southern states were so insistent. The Solicitor General said that he strongly favored the issuance of a decree that would place primary responsibility for implementation on the District Courts, but he also wanted to see the Supreme Court establish specific guidelines. For one thing, the district judges should be told to issue orders requiring the various school boards to submit desegregation plans promptly, with the understanding that any failure to respond within ninety days would result in direct judicial action desegregating the school system at the start of the next academic year. Soboloff maintained that no postponement should be granted by a District Court unless time was required for overcoming legitimate administrative obstacles.[2]

After listening to the arguments on all sides for four days, the Court had to decide how to complete the work that had been left unfinished in 1954. Not too many conferences were required to work out an agreement on the form that the implementation decree should take. Only six weeks after the oral argument—and almost exactly one year after the original decision—the opinion in the second Brown case was handed down. Once again the members of the Court were unanimous in their judgment, and once again Chief Justice Warren was their spokesman.

"All Deliberate Speed"

The implementation plan that Warren announced was similar in many respects to the one that the Justice Department had recommended from the very beginning. Since the Court, unlike a legislative body, could not "pass a law" that would immediately be applicable throughout the country, it would be necessary for private Negro litigants to file suit in order for the desegregation process to begin in any given geographical area. Wherever a suit was instituted, it would be up to the local school board to formulate a desegregation plan that would provide non-discriminatory schooling not only for the particular Negro children who had gone to court but also, in the tradition of "class actions," for all others similarly situated. The school board's plan would be reviewed by the

[2] Sobeloff's moderate position was not moderate enough for the Southerners. When President Eisenhower nominated the Solicitor General in 1955 for a seat on the Court of Appeals for the Fourth Circuit, Southern Senators succeeded in blocking confirmation for a whole year. Although the two Senators from Sobeloff's own state of Maryland supported him, those from the other four states in the Circuit—North Carolina, South Carolina, Virginia, and West Virginia—tried to invoke senatorial courtesy in an effort to prevent confirmation. But senatorial courtesy is not as binding when appellate judgeships are at stake as in the case of District judges, whose jurisdiction extends only to a single state. Not surprisingly, therefore, the Southern maneuvers were all in vain, and Sobeloff was eventually confirmed. *Ibid.*, pp. 23–24.

Federal District Court to ascertain whether it followed the guidelines laid down by the Supreme Court. District judges were ideally suited to perform this function, according to the opinion, "because of their proximity to local conditions."

Foremost among the guidelines established by the Court was the requirement that there be a "prompt and reasonable start toward full compliance." Once such a promising beginning had been made, no time was to be lost. If the school board asked for a breathing spell, it would have to shoulder the burden of proving that the delay it sought was both "necessary in the public interest and . . . consistent with good faith compliance at the earliest practicable date."

Warren said that the existence of bona fide administrative problems would have to be proved by the school board in order to justify any request for delay. Perhaps steps had to be taken to arrange for the transportation of children to new schools, or to reshuffle teaching personnel, or to revise obsolete local laws. Under no circumstance should a postponement be granted merely because of hostile community feeling, for "the vitality of . . . constitutional principles cannot be allowed to yield simply because of disagreement with them." Progress toward total desegregation would have to be made "with all deliberate speed." [3]

It is generally assumed that the term "all deliberate speed" was put into the implementation decree at the suggestion of Justice Frankfurter, who was fond of paradoxes.[4] Whatever

---

[3] *Brown* v. *Board of Education,* 349 U.S. 294 (1955).

[4] Frankfurter may have come across the expression in an opinion that had been written in 1911 by his idol, Oliver Wendell Holmes. In using the words "all deliberate speed," the Great Dissenter had said that he was employing "the language of the English Chancery." This is what he wrote: "A question like the present should be disposed of without undue delay. But a state cannot be expected to move with the celerity of a private businessman; it is enough if it proceeds, in the language of the English Chancery, with all deliberate speed." *Virginia* v. *West Virginia,* 222 U.S. 17, 19–20 (1911). The term "all deliberate speed" is also found in the poem, "Hound of Heaven," by Francis Thompson ("Deliberate speed, majestic instancy") and in Sir Walter Scott's *Rob Roy*. The latter source is the more suggestive one, for Scott was referring to a legal matter. "A suit of law," he wrote, "was forthwith

merits the phrase may have, clarity is certainly not among them. For although "deliberate" is sometimes used in the sense of "intentional," in the more common usage—especially in law—it connotes slowness. Thus, as an adjective modifying "speed," it left something to be desired.

Why had the Court not taken a less ambiguous course and ordered immediate desegregation in the states that were involved in the litigation? A professor of law who was close to Justice Frankfurter has explained that the Justices hoped gradual enforcement would make desegregation more acceptable to a hostile white population in the South.[5] But the Court's implementation decree seemed to encourage the Southern states to experiment with a virtually endless array of devices designed to forestall desegregation. State legislatures passed resolutions purporting to "interpose" the sovereignty of the state between the Supreme Court decision and its enforcement within the boundaries of the state; compulsory school-attendance laws were repealed; public schools were converted into private schools or closed altogether; tuition grants were extended to all-white private schools; the NAACP was outlawed in certain states to complicate the filing of desegregation suits.[6] And in addition to such "legal" devices, direct economic pressure and outright violence were employed against Negroes who were inclined to claim the constitutional rights that the Supreme Court said were theirs. These maneuvers had to be challenged one by one in the courts, making

commenced, and proceeded, as our law-agents assured us, with all deliberate speed." See discussion in Jack Greenberg, *Race Relations and American Law* (New York: Columbia University Press, 1959), pp. 215–17.

[5] Alexander M. Bickel, *The Least Dangerous Branch: The Supreme Court at the Bar of Politics* (Indianapolis: Bobbs-Merrill, 1962), p. 252.

[6] The NAACP has played a vital role in the implementation process. Justice Brennan has explained how: "Typically, a local NAACP branch will invite a member of the legal staff to explain to a meeting of parents and children the legal steps necessary to achieve desegregation. The staff member will bring printed forms to the meeting authorizing him, and other NAACP or Defense Fund attorneys of his designation, to represent the signers in legal proceedings to achieve desegregation." *NAACP* v. *Button,* 371 U.S. 415, 421 (1963).

the advance toward school desegregation agonizingly slow and frustrating.

Foot-dragging by some federal district judges in the South contributed to the long and costly delay. What some judges did, in school cases as well as other civil rights cases, has been described in these words:

> A number of them—although by no means a majority—have again and again ignored ruling precedents of their superior courts which are squarely in point, and have denied Negro plaintiffs the rights to which they are clearly entitled. On being reversed, some have "misinterpreted" the opinion of the appeal courts and entered orders directly at odds with a decision they are obligated to enforce, producing another fruitless round of appeal and remand. Through their control of their court calendars, they have delayed hearing motions or cases for months and, after trial, have refused to decide cases for even longer periods, depriving Negro plaintiffs of even the opportunity to appeal an adverse decision to a higher court.[7]

The Congressional Contribution

The Southern states were further encouraged to make use of delaying techniques because of the attitude adopted by most of their representatives in Congress. Individually as well as collectively, Congressmen from the South launched a campaign to annul the decision of the Supreme Court. Their efforts were climaxed in 1956 by the issuance of a Declaration of Constitutional Principles, signed by more than one hundred Representatives and Senators.[8]

In the strongest terms, the Southern Manifesto, as this document came to be called, recommended that a major effort be made "to bring about a reversal" of the 1954 decision. That

[7] Leon Friedman, "The Federal Courts of the South: Judge Bryan Simpson and His Reluctant Brethren," in Friedman, ed., *Southern Justice* (New York: Pantheon Books, 1965), p. 188.

[8] Only three Southern Senators declined to endorse the Manifesto: Estes Kefauver and Albert Gore of Tennessee, and Lyndon B. Johnson of Texas.

decision, it charged, was devoid of any legal basis and directly "contrary to the Constitution." Not content to condemn the decision that the Court had rendered, the signers of the Manifesto also sought to discredit the Court that had rendered it. The Justices, they said, had been guilty of a "clear abuse of judicial power"; they had "substituted their personal political and social ideas for the established law of the land"; they had exercised "naked judicial power." [9]

The Manifesto endorsed only "lawful means" for reversing the 1954 decision and actually counselled specifically against "disorder and lawless acts." [10] But some of its readers in the South, as might have been expected, were more impressed by the denunciation of the Court and its decision than by the admonition against lawlessness, and it was probably no accident that organizations like the Ku Klux Klan experienced a dramatic revival.

While Southern Congressmen were speaking out against the Court's ruling, Representatives and Senators from the other states were doing little to rally support for the decision in the school cases. Logically, the decision should have been followed by congressional legislation to enforce the constitutional provision that the Court had now reinterpreted. The Constitution, after all, is not self-executing, and the case-by-case adjudication to which the courts are limited is hardly a substitute for legislative implementation of a new national policy.

Yet Congress showed no desire at all to terminate by statute what the Court had said was prohibited by the Constitution. Although a civil rights law was enacted in 1957—the first since the Reconstruction—it said nothing about schools. The next time Congress acted on civil rights, in 1960, there

[9] *Race Relations Law Reporter*, Vol. 1 (April, 1956), pp. 435–36.
[10] In fact, the Manifesto did not really go appreciably beyond what Lincoln had said after the Dred Scott decision: "We do not propose that when Dred Scott has been decided to be a slave by the court, we, as a mob, will decide him to be free . . . ; but we nevertheless do oppose that decision as a political rule. . . . We propose so resisting it as to have it reversed if we can, and a new judicial rule established upon this subject." Quoted in Paul M. Angle, ed., *Created Equal? The Complete Lincoln-Douglas Debates of 1858* (Chicago: University of Chicago Press, 1958), p. 333.

was again no attempt to make a frontal attack on the problem.[11]

Not until 1964—a whole decade after the first Brown decision—was any legislation passed that went to the root of the problem. Faced with the threat of widespread violence as Negroes took to the streets to dramatize their demand for full equality, Congress finally tried to lift the burden of instituting litigation from the shoulders of private Negro litigants, by authorizing the Attorney General to file school desegregation suits in the name of the United States. Moreover, another provision of the law passed in 1964 made it mandatory for the Federal Government to cut off financial support from school systems in which segregation was tolerated.

Presidential Leadership

Just as Congress had sat on its hands for a decade after the school decision, President Eisenhower, too, had refrained from putting the power and prestige of his office behind what the Court had done. Except for urging the District of Columbia to desegregate and thus remove a diplomatic embarrassment, the President never displayed the slightest degree of enthusiasm for the principles enunciated in 1954. Quite the reverse, he was fond of making statements about how difficult it was for law to change the minds of men. Try as he would, he could not bring himself to say anything more positive about the school decision than that it was the law of the land and should be obeyed, like all other laws of the land.

[11] The 1960 law did try to protect federal judges against direct defiance of their orders in school desegregation cases by providing criminal penalties for such conduct. Apart from this, the law dealt with schools in only relatively minor ways: federally subsidized education was authorized for children of military personnel in areas where local schools in only relatively minor ways: federally subsidized education lines after bombing a school was made a federal crime. For a study of this law and the factors that helped account for its ineffectiveness, see Daniel M. Berman, *A Bill Becomes a Law: Congress Enacts Civil Rights Legislation* (New York: Macmillan, 1966), *passim.*

It was not hard to see where Mr. Eisenhower's sympathies lay. The day before the Supreme Court convened for a special term in 1958 to deal with a school integration crisis that had arisen in Little Rock, the President was asked at a press conference about reports that he took a dim view of the original school desegregation decision and was against pushing too fast toward implementation. His response was hardly a model of stylistic clarity, but at least indirect confirmation of the reports seemed to emerge from his words:

> I might have said something about "slower," but I do believe that we should—because I do say, as I did yesterday or last week, we have got to have reason and sense and education, and a lot of other developments that go hand in hand as this process—if this process is going to have any real acceptance in the United States.[12]

With a President sulking in his tent, and with Congress, too, unwilling to act, there was only so much that a Supreme Court could do. Small wonder, then, that even today, despite some progress that has been made during the past few years, token integration of the schools or no integration at all remains the rule in the eleven Southern states, with fewer than 10 percent of the Negro children attending classes with white students. The statistics are even more disheartening for particular areas of the Deep South. In three states, not even 1 percent of the Negro children are studying in integrated situations. The figure is 2 percent in two other states and not quite 3 percent in two more.

It would, however, be seriously misleading to measure the impact of the 1954 school decision in these terms alone. For the ramifications of the decision went far beyond the field of education, or for that matter, the other fields to which the desegregation policy was soon extended. In fact, more than any other single event, the decision helped inspire the epochal

[12] Press conference of August 27, 1958. Ironically, Mr. Eisenhower later found it necessary to send federal troops to Little Rock to enforce a federal court's desegregation order. He was afraid that inaction might lead to a complete breakdown of federal authority.

social and political movement that has accurately been labeled the Negro Revolution. For in essentially unambiguous terms, the Negro was given assurance that the Constitution tolerates no second-class citizenship, thus encouraging him to take whatever action seemed necessary to make practice conform with theory. The Negro was quick to see the point. What ensued was mass action and often civil disobedience, resulting in the creation of an atmosphere in which strong civil rights legislation could be passed and giant steps taken in the direction of a more egalitarian society.

And to the white man the message conveyed by the Court in its decision was equally clear: The line between what America practiced and what it preached would now have to be erased.

Through its 1954 decision the Supreme Court succeeded in forcing into the foreground of public consciousness an issue that America had preferred to forget, and in time its exposition of the relevant constitutional provisions compelled both the Executive and Legislative Branches to grapple with the status of the Negro in American society.

In ruling as it did on school segregation, the Court declined to play the kind of neutral and passive role that some assert to be its only legitimate function in the political system. But the fact remains that passivity cannot always be equated with neutrality. When the Court in 1896, for example, declined to strike down the racial segregation being practiced by Louisiana, it appeared to be taking no action at all. In fact, however, it was in a real sense acting positively, to doom the Negro to degradation and misery as a member of an outcast class.

In some respects, therefore, the Court functioned the same way in both 1896 and 1954, stimulating in each instance a major departure in public policy. The Plessy doctrine pointed the way to a racially segregated society, and the Brown decision to a society devoid of racial discrimination. Accordingly, if judicial lawmaking was involved in 1954, it was likewise involved fifty-eight years earlier. It may follow that those who attack the Brown decision as an intrusion of the judiciary into the policy-making process either lack sufficient understanding of the Court's historic role or else are merely expressing their substantive disagreement with the school segregation decision.

APPENDICES

SUPREME COURT
OF THE UNITED STATES

Oliver Brown, et al.,
Appellants,
1   v.
Board of Education of To-
peka, Shawnee County,
Kansas, et al.

On Appeal From the
United States District
Court for the District
of Kansas.

Harry Briggs, Jr., et al.,
Appellants,
2   v.
R. W. Elliott, et al.

On Appeal From the
United States District
Court for the Eastern
District of South Caro-
lina.

Dorothy E. Davis, et al.,
Appellants,
4   v.
County School Board of
Prince Edward County,
Virginia, et al.

On Appeal From the
United States District
Court for the Eastern
District of Virginia.

Francis B. Gebhart, et al.,
Petitioners,
10   v.
Ethel Louise Belton, et al.

On Writ of Certiorari to
the Supreme Court of
Delaware.

[May 17, 1954.]
(347 U.S. 483)

MR. CHIEF JUSTICE WARREN delivered the opinion of the
Court.

133

These cases come to us from the States of Kansas, South Carolina, Virginia, and Delaware. They are premised on different facts and different local conditions, but a common legal question justifies their consideration together in this consolidated opinion.[1]

In each of the cases, minors of the Negro race, through their legal representatives, seek the aid of the courts in obtaining admission to the public schools of their community on a nonsegregated basis. In each instance, they had been denied

[1] In the Kansas case, *Brown* v. *Board of Education,* the plaintiffs are Negro children of elementary school age residing in Topeka. They brought this action in the United States District Court for the District of Kansas to enjoin enforcement of a Kansas statute which permits, but does not require, cities of more than 15,000 population to maintain separate school facilities for Negro and white students. Kan. Gen. Stat. § 72-1724 (1949). Pursuant to that authority, the Topeka Board of Education elected to establish segregated elementary schools. Other public schools in the community, however, are operated on a nonsegregated basis. The three-judge District Court, convened under 28 U.S.C. §§ 2281 and 2284, found that segregation in public education has a detrimental effect upon Negro children, but denied relief on the ground that the Negro and white schools were substantially equal with respect to buildings, transportation, curricula, and educational qualifications of teachers. 98 F. Supp. 797. The case is here on direct appeal under 28 U.S.C. § 1253.

In the South Carolina case, *Briggs* v. *Elliott,* the plaintiffs are Negro children of both elementary and high school age residing in Clarendon County. They brought this action in the United States District Court for the Eastern District of South Carolina to enjoin enforcement of provisions in the state constitution and statutory code which require the segregation of Negroes and whites in public schools. S. C. Const., Art. XI, § 7; S. C. Code § 5377 (1942). The three-judge District Court, convened under 28 U.S.C. §§ 2281 and 2284, denied the requested relief. The court found that the Negro schools were inferior to the white schools and ordered the defendants to begin immediately to equalize the facilities. But the court sustained the validity of the contested provisions and denied the plaintiffs admission to the white schools during the equalization program. 98 F. Supp. 529. This Court vacated the District Court's judgment and remanded the case for the purpose of obtaining the court's views on a report filed by the defendants concerning the progress made in the equalization program. 342 U.S. 350. On remand, the District Court found that substantial equality had been achieved except for buildings and that the defendants were proceeding to rectify this inequality as well. 103 F. Supp. 920. The case is again here on direct appeal under 28 U.S.C. § 1253.

admission to schools attended by white children under laws requiring or permitting segregation according to race. This segregation was alleged to deprive the plaintiffs of the equal protection of the laws under the Fourteenth Amendment. In each of the cases other than the Delaware case, a three-judge federal district court denied relief to the plaintiffs on the so-called "separate but equal" doctrine announced by this Court in *Plessy* v. *Ferguson,* 163 U.S. 537. Under that doctrine,

---

In the Virginia case, *Davis* v. *County School Board,* the plaintiffs are Negro children of high school age residing in Prince Edward County. They brought this action in the United States District Court for the Eastern District of Virginia to enjoin enforcement of provisions in the state constitution and statutory code which require the segregation of Negroes and whites in public schools. Va. Const., § 140; Va. Code § 22-221 (1950). The three-judge District Court, convened under 28 U.S.C. §§ 2281 and 2284, denied the requested relief. The court found the Negro school inferior in physical plant, curricula, and transportation, and ordered the defendants forthwith to provide substantially equal curricula and transportation and to "proceed with all reasonable diligence and dispatch to remove" the inequality in physical plant. But, as in the South Carolina case, the court sustained the validity of the contested provisions and denied the plaintiffs admission to the white schools during the equalization program. 103 F. Supp. 337. The case is here on direct appeal under 28 U.S.C. § 1253.

In the Delaware case, *Gebhart* v. *Belton,* the plaintiffs are Negro children of both elementary and high school age residing in New Castle County. They brought this action in the Delaware Court of Chancery to enjoin enforcement of provisions in the state constitution and statutory code which require the segregation of Negroes and whites in public schools. Del. Const., Art. X, § 2; Del. Rev. Code § 2631 (1935). The Chancellor gave judgment for the plaintiffs and ordered their immediate admission to schools previously attended only by white children, on the ground that the Negro schools were inferior with respect to teacher training, pupil-teacher ratio, extra-curricular activities, physical plant, and time and distance involved in travel. 87 A. 2d 862. The Chancellor also found that segregation itself results in an inferior education for Negro children (see note 10, *infra*), but did not rest his decision on that ground. *Id.,* at 865. The Chancellor's decree was affirmed by the Supreme Court of Delaware, which intimated, however, that the defendants might be able to obtain a modification of the decree after equalization of the Negro and white schools had been accomplished. 91 A. 2d 137, 152. The defendants, contending only that the Delaware courts had erred in ordering the immediate admission of the Negro plaintiffs to the white schools, applied to this Court for certiorari. The writ was granted, 344 U.S. 891. The plaintiffs, who were successful below, did not submit a cross-petition.

equality of treatment is accorded when the races are provided substantially equal facilities, even though these facilities be separate. In the Delaware case, the Supreme Court of Delaware adhered to that doctrine, but ordered that the plaintiffs be admitted to the white schools because of their superiority to the Negro schools.

The plaintiffs contend that segregated public schools are not "equal" and cannot be made "equal," and that hence they are deprived of the equal protection of the laws. Because of the obvious importance of the question presented, the Court took jurisdiction.[2] Argument was heard in the 1952 Term, and reargument was heard this Term on certain questions propounded by the Court.[3]

Reargument was largely devoted to the circumstances surrounding the adoption of the Fourteenth Amendment in 1868. It covered exhaustively consideration of the Amendment in Congress, ratification by the states, then existing practices in racial segregation, and the views of proponents and opponents of the Amendment. This discussion and our own investigation convince us that, although these sources cast some light, it is not enough to resolve the problem with which we are faced. At best, they are inconclusive. The most avid proponents of the post-War Amendments undoubtedly intended them to remove all legal distinctions among "all persons born or naturalized in the United States." Their opponents, just as certainly, were antagonistic to both the letter and the spirit of the Amendments and wished them to have the most limited effect. What others in Congress and the state legislatures had in mind cannot be determined with any degree of certainty.

An additional reason for the inconclusive nature of the Amendment's history, with respect to segregated schools, is the status of public education at that time.[4] In the South, the movement toward free common schools, supported by general

[2] 334 U.S. 1, 141, 891.

[3] 345 U.S. 972. The Attorney General of the United States participated both Terms as *amicus curiae*.

[4] For a general study of the development of public education prior to the Amendment, see Butts and Cremin, A History of Education in

taxation, had not yet taken hold. Education of white children was largely in the hands of private groups. Education of Negroes was almost nonexistent, and practically all of the race were illiterate. In fact, any education of Negroes was forbidden by law in some states. Today, in contrast, many Negroes have achieved outstanding success in the arts and sciences as well as in the business and professional world. It is true that public education had already advanced further in the North, but the effect of the Amendment on Northern States was generally ignored in the congressional debates. Even in the North, the conditions of public education did not approximate those existing today. The curriculum was usually rudimentary; ungraded schools were common in rural areas; the school term was but three months a year in many states; and compulsory school attendance was virtually unknown. As a consequence, it is not surprising that there should be so little in the history of the Fourteenth Amendment relating to its intended effect on public education.

In the first cases in this Court construing the Fourteenth Amendment, decided shortly after its adoption, the Court

American Culture (1953), Pts. I, II; Cubberley, Public Education in the United States (1934 ed.), cc. II–XII. School practices current at the time of the adoption of the Fourteenth Amendment are described in Butts and Crimen, *supra*, at 269–275; Cubberley, *supra*, at 288–339, 408–431; Knight, Public Education in the South (1922), cc. VIII, IX. See also H. Ex. Doc. No. 315, 41st Cong., 2d Sess. (1871). Although the demand for free public schools followed substantially the same pattern in both the North and the South, the development in the South did not begin to gain momentum until about 1850, some twenty years after that in the North. The reasons for the somewhat slower development in the South (*e. g.*, the rural character of the South and the different regional attitudes toward state assistance) are well explained in Cubberley, *supra*, at 408–423. In the country as a whole, but particularly in the South, the War virtually stopped all progress in public education. *Id.*, at 427–428. The low status of Negro education in all sections of the country, both before and immediately after the War, is described in Beale, A History of Freedom of Teaching in American Schools (1941), 112–132, 175–195. Compulsory school attendance laws were not generally adopted until after the ratification of the Fourteenth Amendment, and it was not until 1918 that such laws were in force in all the states. Cubberley, *supra*, at 563–565.

interpreted it as proscribing all state-imposed discriminations against the Negro race.[5] The doctrine of "separate but equal" did not make its appearance in this court until 1896 in the case of *Plessy* v. *Ferguson, supra,* involving not education but transportation.[6] American courts have since labored with the doctrine for over half a century. In this Court, there have been six cases involving the "separate but equal" doctrine in the field of public education.[7] In *Cumming* v. *County Board of Education,* 175 U.S. 528, and *Gong Lum* v. *Rice,* 275 U.S. 78, the validity of the doctrine itself was not challenged.[8] In more recent cases, all on the graduate school level, inequality was

---

[5] *Slaughter-House Cases,* 16 Wall. 36, 67–72 (1873); *Strauder* v. *West Virginia,* 100 U.S. 303, 307–308 (1879):

"It ordains that no State shall deprive any person of life, liberty, or property, without due process of law, or deny to any person within its jurisdiction the equal protection of the laws. What is this but declaring that the law in the States shall be the same for the black as for the white; that all persons, whether colored or white, shall stand equal before the laws of the States, and, in regard to the colored race, for whose protection the amendment was primarily designed, that no discrimination shall be made against them by law because of their color? The words of the amendment, it is true, are prohibitory, but they contain a necessary implication of a positive immunity, or right, most valuable to the colored race,—the right to exemption from unfriendly legislation against them distinctively as colored,—exemption from legal discriminations, implying inferiority in civil society, lessening the security of their enjoyment of the rights which others enjoy, and discriminations which are steps towards reducing them to the condition of a subject race."

See also *Virginia* v. *Rives,* 100 U.S. 313, 318 (1879); Ex parte *Virginia,* 100 U.S. 339, 344–345 (1879).

[6] The doctrine apparently originated in *Roberts* v. *City of Boston,* 59 Mass. 198, 206 (1849), upholding school segregation against attack as being violative of a state constitutional guarantee of equality. Segregation in Boston public schools was eliminated in 1855. Mass. Acts 1855, c. 256. But elsewhere in the North segregation in public education has persisted until recent years. It is apparent that such segregation has long been a nationwide problem, not merely one of sectional concern.

[7] See also *Berea College* v. *Kentucky,* 211 U.S. 45 (1908).

[8] In the *Cumming* case, Negro taxpayers sought an injunction requiring the defendant school board to discontinue the operation of a high school for white children until the board resumed operation of a high school for Negro children. Similarly, in the *Gong Lum* case, the plaintiff, a child of Chinese descent, contended only that state authorities had misapplied the doctrine by classifying him with Negro children and requiring him to attend a Negro school.

found in that specific benefits enjoyed by white students were denied to Negro students of the same educational qualifications. *Missouri* ex rel. *Gaines* v. *Canada,* 305 U.S. 337; *Sipuel* v. *Oklahoma,* 332 U.S. 631; *Sweatt* v. *Painter,* 339 U.S. 629; *McLaurin* v. *Oklahoma State Regents,* 339 U.S. 637. In none of these cases was it necessary to reexamine the doctrine to grant relief to the Negro plaintiff. And in *Sweatt* v. *Painter, supra,* the Court expressly reserved decision on the question whether *Plessy* v. *Ferguson* should be held inapplicable to public education.

In the instant cases, that question is directly presented. Here, unlike *Sweatt* v. *Painter,* there are findings below that the Negro and white schools involved have been equalized, or are being equalized, with respect to buildings, curricula, qualifications and salaries of teachers, and other "tangible" factors.[9] Our decision, therefore, cannot turn on merely a comparison of these tangible factors in the Negro and white schools involved in each of the cases. We must look instead to the effect of segregation itself on public education.

In approaching this problem, we cannot turn the clock back to 1868 when the Amendment was adopted, or even to 1896 when *Plessy* v. *Ferguson* was written. We must consider public education in the light of its full development and its present place in American life throughout the Nation. Only in this way can it be determined if segregation in public schools deprives these plaintiffs of the equal protection of the laws.

Today, education is perhaps the most important function of state and local governments. Compulsory school attendance

[9] In the Kansas case, the court below found substantial equality as to all such factors. 98 F. Supp. 797, 798. In the South Carolina case, the court below found that the defendants were proceeding "promptly and in good faith to comply with the court's decree." 103 F. Supp. 920, 921. In the Virginia case, the court below noted that the equalization program was already "afoot and progressing" (103 F. Supp. 337, 341); since then, we have been advised, in the Virginia Attorney General's brief on reargument, that the program has now been completed. In the Delaware case, the court below similarly noted that the state's equalization program was well under way. 91 A. 2d 137, 149.

laws and the great expenditures for education both demonstrate our recognition of the importance of education to our democratic society. It is required in the performance of our most basic public responsibilities, even service in the armed forces. It is the very foundation of good citizenship. Today it is a principal instrument in awakening the child to cultural values, in preparing him for later professional training, and in helping him to adjust normally to his environment. In these days, it is doubtful that any child may reasonably be expected to succeed in life if he is denied the opportunity of an education. Such an opportunity, where the state has undertaken to provide it, is a right which must be made available to all on equal terms.

We come then to the question presented: Does segregation of children in public schools solely on the basis of race, even though the physical facilities and other "tangible" factors may be equal, deprive the children of the minority group of equal education opportunities? We believe that it does.

In *Sweatt* v. *Painter, supra,* in finding that a segregated law school for Negroes could not provide them equal educational opportunities, this Court relied in large part on "those qualities which are incapable of objective measurement but which make for greatness in a law school." In *McLaurin* v. *Oklahoma State Regents, supra,* the Court, in requiring that a Negro admitted to a white graduate school be treated like all other students, again resorted to intangible considerations: ". . . his ability to study, to engage in discussions and exchange views with other students, and, in general, to learn his profession." Such considerations apply with added force to children in grade and high schools. To separate them from others of similar age and qualifications solely because of their race generates a feeling of inferiority as to their status in the community that may affect their hearts and minds in a way unlikely ever to be undone. The effect of this separation on their educational opportunities was well stated by a finding in the Kansas case by a court which nevertheless felt compelled to rule against the Negro plaintiffs:

"Segregation of white and colored children in public schools has a detrimental effect upon the colored children. The impact is greater when it has the sanction of the law; for the policy of separating the races is usually interpreted as denoting the inferiority of the Negro group. A sense of inferiority affects the motivation of a child to learn. Segregation with the sanction of law, therefore, has a tendency to retard the educational and mental development of Negro children and to deprive them of some of the benefits they would receive in a racially integrated school system." [10]

Whatever may have been the extent of psychological knowledge at the time of *Plessy* v. *Ferguson,* this finding is amply supported by modern authority.[11] Any language in *Plessy* v. *Ferguson* contrary to this finding is rejected.

We conclude that in the field of public education the doctrine of "separate but equal" has no place. Separate educational facilities are inherently unequal. Therefore, we hold that the plaintiffs and others similarly situated for whom the actions have been brought are, by reason of the segregation complained of, deprived of the equal protection of the laws guaranteed by the Fourteenth Amendment. This disposition makes unnecessary any discussion whether such segregation also violates the Due Process Clause of the Fourteenth Amendment.[12]

[10] A similar finding was made in the Delaware case: "I conclude from the testimony that in our Delaware society, State-imposed segregation in education itself results in the Negro children, as a class, receiving educational opportunities which are substantially inferior to those available to white children otherwise similarly situated." 87 A. 2d 862, 865.

[11] K. B. Clark, Effect of Prejudice and Discrimination on Personality Development (Midcentury White House Conference on Children and Youth, 1950); Witmer and Kotinsky, Personality in the Making (1952), c. VI; Deutscher and Chein, The Psychological Effects of Enforced Segregation: A Survey of Social Science Opinion, 26 J. Psychol. 259 (1948); Chein, What are the Psychological Effects of Segregation Under Conditions of Equal Facilities?, 3 Int. J. Opinion and Attitude Res. 229 (1949); Brameld, Educational Costs, in Discrimination and National Welfare (McIver, ed., 1949), 44–48; Frazier, The Negro in the United States (1949), 674–681. And see generally Myrdal, An American Dilemma (1944).

[12] See *Bolling* v. *Sharpe, infra,* concerning the Due Process Clause of the Fifth Amendment.

Because these are class actions, because of the wide applicability of this decision, and because of the great variety of local conditions, the formulation of decrees in these cases presents problems of considerable complexity. On reargument, the consideration of appropriate relief was necessarily subordinated to the primary question—the constitutionality of segregation in public education. We have now announced that such segregation is a denial of the equal protection of the laws. In order that we may have the full assistance of the parties in formulating decrees, the cases will be restored to the docket, and the parties are requested to present further argument on Questions 4 and 5 previously propounded by the Court for the reargument this Term.[13] The Attorney General of the United States is again invited to participate. The Attorneys General of the states requiring or permitting segregation in public education will also be permitted to appear as *amici curiae* upon request to do so by September 15, 1954, and submission of briefs by October 1, 1954.[14]

It is so ordered.

[13] "4. Assuming it is decided that segregation in public schools violates the Fourteenth Amendment.

"(a) would a decree necessarily follow providing that, within the limits set by normal geographic school districting, Negro children should forthwith be admitted to schools of their choice, or

"(b) may this Court, in the exercise of its equity powers, permit an effective gradual adjustment to be brought about from existing segregated systems to a system not based on color distinctions?

"5. On the assumption on which questions 4 (a) and (b) are based, and assuming further that this Court will exercise its equity powers to the end described in question 4 (b),

"(a) should this Court formulate detailed decrees in these cases;

"(b) if so, what specific issues should the decrees reach;

"(c) should this Court appoint a special master to hear evidence with a view to recommending specific terms for such decrees;

"(d) should this Court remand to the courts of first instance with directions to frame decrees in these cases, and if so, what general directions should the decrees of this Court include and what procedures should the courts of first instance follow in arriving at the specific terms of more detailed decrees?"

[14] See Rule 42, Revised Rules of this Court (effective July 1, 1954).

SUPREME COURT
OF THE UNITED STATES

No. 8—October Term, 1953.

| Spottswood Thomas Bolling, et al., Petitioners, v. C. Melvin Sharpe, et al. | On Writ of Certiorari to the United States Court of Appeals for the District of Columbia Circuit. |

[May 17, 1954.]

(347 U.S. 497)

Mr. Chief Justice Warren delivered the opinion of the Court.

This case challenges the validity of segregation in the public schools of the District of Columbia. The petitioners, minors of the Negro race, allege that such segregation deprives them of due process of law under the Fifth Amendment. They were refused admission to a public school attended by white children solely because of their race. They sought the aid of the District Court for the District of Columbia in obtaining admission. That court dismissed their complaint. We granted a writ of certiorari before judgment in the Court of Appeals because of the importance of the constitutional question presented: 344 U.S. 873.

We have this day held that the Equal Protection Clause of the Fourteenth Amendment prohibits the states from maintaining racially segregated public schools.[1] The legal problem

[1] *Brown* v. *Board of Education,* 347 U.S. 483.

in the District of Columbia is somewhat different, however. The Fifth Amendment, which is applicable in the District of Columbia, does not contain an equal protection clause as does the Fourteenth Amendment which applies only to the states. But the concepts of equal protection and due process, both stemming from our American ideal of fairness, are not mutually exclusive. The "equal protection of the laws" is a more explicit safeguard of prohibited unfairness than "due process of law," and, therefore, we do not imply that the two are always interchangeable phrases. But, as this Court has recognized, discrimination may be so unjustifiable as to be violative of due process.[2]

Classifications based solely upon race must be scrutinized with particular care, since they are contrary to our traditions and hence constitutionally suspect.[3] As long ago as 1896, this Court declared the principle "that the Constitution of the United States, in its present form, forbids, so far as civil and political rights are concerned, discrimination by the General Government, or by the States, against any citizen because of his race." [4] And in *Buchanan* v. *Warley*, 245 U.S. 60, the Court held that a statute which limited the right of a property owner to convey his property to a person of another race was, as an unreasonable discrimination, a denial of due process of law.

Although the Court has not assumed to define "liberty" with any great precision, that term is not confined to mere freedom from bodily restraint. Liberty under law extends to the full range of conduct which the individual is free to pursue, and it cannot be restricted except for a proper governmental objective. Segregation in public education is not reasonably related to any proper governmental objective, and thus it imposes on Negro children of the District of Columbia a burden that constitutes an arbitrary deprivation of their liberty in

---

[2] *Detroit Bank* v. *United States,* 317 U.S. 329; *Currin* v. *Wallace,* 306 U.S. 1, 13–14; *Steward Machine Co.* v. *Davis,* 301 U.S. 548, 585.

[3] *Korematsu* v. *United States,* 323 U.S. 214, 216; *Hirabayashi* v. *United States,* 320 U.S. 81, 100.

[4] *Gibson* v. *Mississippi,* 162 U.S. 565, 591. Cf. *Steel* v. *Louisville & Nashville R. Co.,* 323 U.S. 192, 198–199.

violation of the Due Process Clause.

In view of our decision that the Constitution prohibits the states from maintaining racially segregated public schools, it would be unthinkable that the same Constitution would impose a lesser duty on the Federal Government.[5] We hold that racial segregation in the public schools of the District of Columbia is a denial of the due process of law guaranteed by the Fifth Amendment to the Constitution.

For the reasons set out in *Brown* v. *Board of Education*, this case will be restored to the docket for reargument on Questions 4 and 5 previously propounded by the Court. 345 U.S. 972.

It is so ordered.

[5] Cf. *Hurd* v. *Hodge,* 334 U.S. 24.

SUPREME COURT
OF THE UNITED STATES

BROWN ET AL. *v.* BOARD OF EDUCATION
OF TOPEKA ET AL.

(349 U.S. 294 [1955])

NO. 1. APPEAL FROM THE UNITED STATES DISTRICT COURT
FOR THE DISTRICT OF KANSAS.*

Reargued on the question of relief April 11–14, 1955.—Opinion
and judgments announced May 31, 1955.

MR. CHIEF JUSTICE WARREN delivered the opinion of the
Court.

These cases were decided on May 17, 1954. The opinions
of that date,[1] declaring the fundamental principle that racial
discrimination in public education is unconstitutional, are
incorporated herein by reference. All provisions of federal,
state, or local law requiring or permitting such discrimination
must yield to this principle. There remains for consideration
the manner in which relief is to be accorded.

Because these cases arose under different local conditions
and their disposition will involve a variety of local problems,

---

* Together with No. 2, *Briggs et al.* v. *Elliott et al.*, on appeal from
the United States District Court for the Eastern District of South Carolina; No. 3, *Davis et al.* v. *County School Board of Prince Edward County,
Virginia, et al.*, on appeal from the United States District Court for the
Eastern District of Virginia; No. 4, *Bolling et al.* v. *Sharpe et al.*, on
certiorari to the United States Court of Appeals for the District of Columbia Circuit; and No. 5, *Gebhart et al.* v. *Belton et al.*, on certiorari to
the Supreme Court of Delaware.

[1] 347 U.S. 483; 347 U.S. 497.

we requested further argument on the question of relief.[2] In view of the nationwide importance of the decision, we invited the Attorney General of the United States and the Attorneys General of all states requiring or permitting racial discrimination in public education to present their views on that question. The parties, the United States, and the States of Florida, North Carolina, Arkansas, Oklahoma, Maryland, and Texas filed briefs and participated in the oral argument.

These presentations were informative and helpful to the Court in its consideration of the complexities arising from the transition to a system of public education freed of racial discrimination. The presentations also demonstrated that substantial steps to eliminate racial discrimination in public schools have already been taken, not only in some of the communities in which these cases arose, but in some of the states appearing as *amici curiae,* and in other states as well. Substantial progress has been made in the District of Columbia and in the communities in Kansas and Delaware involved in this litigation. The defendants in the cases coming to us from South Carolina and Virginia are awaiting the decision of this

[2] Further argument was requested on the following questions, 347 U.S. 483, 495–496, n. 13, previously propounded by the Court:

"4. Assuming it is decided that segregation in public schools violates the Fourteenth Amendment

"(a) would a decree necessarily follow providing that, within the limits set by normal geographic school districting, Negro children should forthwith be admitted to schools of their choice, or

"(b) may this court, in the exercise of its equity powers, permit an effective gradual adjustment to be brought about from existing segregated systems to a system not based on color distinctions?

"5. On the assumption on which questions 4 (a) and (b) are based, and assuming further that this Court will exercise its equity powers to the end described in question 4 (b),

"(a) should this Court formulate detailed decrees in these cases;

"(b) if so, what specific issues should the decrees reach;

"(c) should this Court appoint a special master to hear evidence with a view to recommending specific terms for such decrees;

"(d) should this Court remand to the courts of first instance with directions to frame decrees in these cases, and if so what general directions should the decrees of this Court include and what procedures should the courts of first instance follow in arriving at the specific terms of more detailed decrees?"

Court concerning relief.

Full implementation of these constitutional principles may require solution of varied local school problems. School authorities have the primary responsibility for elucidating, assessing, and solving these problems; courts will have to consider whether the action of school authorities constitutes good faith implementation of the governing constitutional principles. Because of their proximity to local conditions and the possible need for further hearings, the courts which originally heard these cases can best perform this judicial appraisal. Accordingly, we believe it appropriate to remand the cases to those courts.[3]

In fashioning and effectuating the decrees, the courts will be guided by equitable principles. Traditionally, equity has been characterized by a practical flexibility in shaping its remedies[4] and by a facility for adjusting and reconciling public and private needs.[5] These cases call for the exercise of these traditional attributes of equity power. At stake is the personal interest of the plaintiffs in admission to public schools as soon as practicable on a nondiscriminatory basis. To effectuate this interest may call for elimination of a variety of obstacles in making the transition to school systems operated in accordance with the constitutional principles set forth in our May 17, 1954, decision. Courts of equity may properly take into account the public interest in the elimination of such obstacles in a systematic and effective manner. But it should go without saying that the vitality of these constitutional principles cannot be allowed to yield simply because of disagreement with them.

While giving weight to these public and private considerations, the courts will require that the defendants make a prompt and reasonable start toward full compliance with

[3] The cases coming to us from Kansas, South Carolina, and Virginia were originally heard by three-judge District Courts convened under 28 U.S.C. §§ 2281 and 2284. These cases will accordingly be remanded to those three-judge courts. See *Briggs* v. *Elliott*, 342 U.S. 350.

[4] See *Alexander* v. *Hillman*, 296 U.S. 222, 239.

[5] See *Hecht Co.* v. *Bowles*, 321 U.S. 321, 329–330.

our May 17, 1954, ruling. Once such a start has been made, the courts may find that additional time is necessary to carry out the ruling in an effective manner. The burden rests upon the defendants to establish that such time is necessary in the public interest and is consistent with good faith compliance at the earliest practicable date. To that end, the courts may consider problems related to administration, arising from the physical condition of the school plant, the school transportation system, personnel, revision of school districts and attendance areas into compact units to achieve a system of determining admission to the public schools on a nonracial basis, and revision of local laws and regulations which may be necessary in solving the foregoing problems. They will also consider the adequacy of any plans the defendants may propose to meet these problems and to effectuate a transition to a racially nondiscriminatory school system. During this period of transition, the courts will retain jurisdiction of these cases.

The judgments below, except that in the Delaware case, are accordingly reversed and the cases are remanded to the District Courts to take such proceedings and enter such orders and decrees consistent with this opinion as are necessary and proper to admit to public schools on a racially nondiscriminatory basis with all deliberate speed the parties to these cases. The judgment in the Delaware case—ordering the immediate admission of the plaintiffs to schools previously attended only by white children—is affirmed on the basis of the principles stated in our May 17, 1954, opinion, but the case is remanded to the Supreme Court of Delaware for such further proceedings as that Court may deem necessary in light of this opinion.

It is so ordered.

INDEX OF JURIDICAL TERMS

GENERAL INDEX

INDEX OF JURIDICAL TERMS

[In this specialized index, supplementing the General Index that follows, the page references in each case are to the portions of the text containing the most direct definition or description of the particular term.]

GENERAL INDEX